BILLY
CONNOLLY

BILLY CONNOLLY

The unofficial and unauthorised biography of
BILLY CONNOLLY
by Nigel Huddleston

Published by
Kandour Ltd
1-3 Colebrook Place
London N1 8HZ

This edition printed in 2004 for
Bookmart Limited
Registered Number 2372865
Trading as Bookmart Ltd
Blaby Road
Wigston
Leicester LE18 4SE

First published June 2004

ISBN 1–904756–02–6

Production services:
Metro Media Ltd

Author: Nigel Huddleston

With thanks to: Jenny Ross, Emma Hayley,
Lee Coventry, Belinda Weber

Cover design: Mike Lomax
Cover Image: Rex Features

Inside Images: Rex Features

© Kandour Ltd

Printed and bound by Nørhaven Paperback, Denmark

BILLY CONNOLLY

FOREWORD

This series of biographies is a celebration of celebrity. It features some of the world's greatest modern-day icons including movie stars, soap personalities, pop idols, comedians and sporting heroes. Each biography examines their struggles, their family background, their rise to stardom and in some cases their struggle to stay there. The books aim to shed some light on what makes a star. Why do some people succeed when others fail?

Written in a light-hearted and lively way, and coupled with the most up-to-date details on the world's favourite heroes and heroines, this series is an entertaining read for anyone interested in the world of celebrity. Discover all about their career highlights – what was the defining moment to propel them into superstardom? No story about fame is without its ups and downs. We reveal the emotional rollercoaster ride that many of these stars have been on to stay at the top. Read all about your most adored personalities in these riveting books.

BILLY CONNOLLY

CONTENTS

BILLY CONNOLLY

Full name: William Connolly
Eye colour: Brown
Date of birth: 24 November 1942
Place of birth: Glasgow, Scotland

Marriages: Iris Pressagh (1969–1985, separated in 1981): Pamela Stephenson (1989– present day)

Children:
Son: James (Jamie); mother Iris Pessagh, born 1969
Daughter: Cara; mother Iris Pressagh, born 1973
Daughter: Daisy; mother Pamela Stephenson, born 1983
Daughter: Amy; mother Pamela Stephenson, born 1986
Daughter: Scarlett; mother Pamela Stephenson, born 1988

Star sign: Sagittarius (23 November to 22 December)
Sagittarians are warm, caring, gregarious, optimistic and outgoing. They like their freedom but make relationships as much fun as possible. They're

FACT FILE

also curious and open-minded and like to learn about other people. However, they can tend to speak their mind without thinking about other people's feelings! Other famous Sagittarians include Uri Geller, Winston Churchill and Britney Spears.

Chinese birth sign: Horse
Cheerful, well-liked and unpredictable. They are independent, fair-minded and adaptable with great powers of persuasion. They tend to have a lot of friends but prefer to be self-reliant.

Career highlights:
First *Parkinson* show in 1975; the film *Mrs Brown* with Dame Judi Dench in 1997.

1

Introduction

BILLY CONNOLLY

INTRODUCTION

I t's August 2003 and Billy Connolly is 30,000 feet above the ground. He's returning from New Zealand where he's been promoting a film and playing gigs for the latest installment of his *World Tour* TV shows. Unusually for someone who's built a career around talking about willies, among other things, he hasn't checked his flies. When he glances down, he notices they're undone and decides to do the decent thing. Moments later he's writhing in agony and has drawn blood – he's got his willy caught in his zip. "I was sitting on the flight and I noticed my flies were undone, so obviously I didn't want to give anyone a fright," the

BILLY CONNOLLY

INTRODUCTION

Daily Record reported him as saying. He went on, "It was absolute agony but, however tempted you may be, you just can't ask the stewardess for help."

The person he should have turned to was in fact... Billy Connolly. If the findings of a group of academics in his hometown are anything to go by, the Big Yin could have soothed the pain by talking to himself. A study by psychology professors at Glasgow Caledonian University, in conjunction with the Scottish Network for Chronic Pain Research, found that listening to Billy Connolly routines can act as a painkiller, increasing tolerance by up to three times. Try telling that to Michael Parkinson, who claims he once had to leave the auditorium at a Billy Connolly concert because his sides were aching with laughter.

Although it hurt at the time, Connolly will no doubt come to see the funny side of the flying flies incident, and the news that he's become a sort of comic anaesthetic will no doubt cause some amusement too. In fact they're the sorts of weird human life events that Connolly draws on for his routines when they happen to other people. Material comes flying in from every corner: his own childhood (the staccato delivery of an angry parent: "don't ... you ... ever ... do ... that ... again"); irritating TV

INTRODUCTION

presenters ("There's no such thing as bad weather, only the wrong clothes. Get yourself a sexy raincoat and live a little"); the Scottish corporate inferiority complex ("Scotland has the only football team in the world that does a lap of disgrace"); and more latterly, his own children ("Don't buy one of those baby intercoms. Babies pretend to be dead. They're bastards and they do it on purpose"). He finds mirth in the most unexpected places, often from the misfortune of himself or others. A routine begun in his Fifties concerns the propensity of Connolly's doctor to explore his anus with his finger once he'd reached middle age. In a BBC interview to promote his 2001 film *The Man Who Sued God*, he said: "Extreme discomfort, like having no trousers when everyone else has got their's on, is funny."

Sometimes, bits of the routine are simply made up on the spot, or more probably, judging by the startled "where did that come from?" grin that comes over his face, they just flash into his mind. "There are nights when nothing comes into your head," he told the BBC in August 2003. "You can't stand there staring at them so you've got to have this body of work that has a shape, but the trick is to surround it with everything that comes into

INTRODUCTION

your head." More than once he's said that he sometimes wished he'd been in his own audience because he'd done so much new stuff off-the-cuff.

In another 2003 interview he said: "Other comics cannot believe that I do not write. Most of them write it, learn it and talk it, but I don't. I have stories that I remember and I add or subtract as I go along". He added, "I go out with an opening line, the audience settles down knowing it is going to be politically incorrect and rebellious. That has been the way it has been and, so far, every decade has been better than the last."

Ask anyone to list some of the British comedy greats and there are going to be some inevitable names near the top of the list: Morecambe and Wise, the double act with the biggest British TV viewing figures outside of state and sporting occasions; Peter Cook, the genius wit with the masterful ad-lib; Tommy Cooper, the misfit magician who could make an audience howl just by walking on stage. But there's one man in the last 30 years who has had the global fan base that Eric and Ernie never had; who can improvise routines around everyday life and take them to surreal places Cook could never dream of; and whose patent big banana boots, leotards and straggling

BILLY CONNOLLY

INTRODUCTION

beard make Cooper's tufty hair and fez look tame. And if you consider that that performer also has the physicality of Lee Evans, the sauciness of Benny Hill and the sofa-chumminess of Graham Norton, it's only fair that Billy Connolly should top a 2003 London Comedy Poll to find Britain's favourite comedian.

All the other comics mentioned so far were in the top 10, but it's more than just Billy Connolly's all-round comic genius that puts him head and shoulders above the rest. Connolly has also proved himself to be an accomplished serious actor with dozens of small- and big-screen chalk marks to his name. In 2003, he could be seen putting Tom Cruise on the road to nineteenth-century-Japan in *The Last Samurai* and is reported to be in line to earn $1 million to appear alongside Meryl Streep and Jim Carrey in a forthcoming children's blockbuster.

And unlike the rest of the British comic royalty, Connolly cut the mustard in the USA, "breaking" that market in a way that chart-topping pop groups since The Beatles and the Stones have invariably failed to do, let alone mere stand-up comedians. Of course, like The Beatles and the Stones, Billy Connolly has been to the top of the pop charts too with D.I.V.O.R.C.E. in 1975,

INTRODUCTION

just in case you thought there was a corner of show business he'd left unexplored. That was back in the days when to have a number one hit took either effort or genius (or both), rather than a marketing plan like an American war strategy.

On the way he's experienced heartache of his own with an abusive childhood and a D.I.V.O.R.C.E. of his own, found the time and energy to bring up five children, been hounded by the press on more than one occasion, and faced up to some considerable inner demons. But Billy Connolly is a survivor. Now in his 60s, he's been in show business for all of 40 years, and 2004 finds him still touring. When he started out Milligan and Morecambe were his contemporaries; these days it's Merton and Reeves and Mortimer – and it's a tribute to the timelessness of Connolly's observations on life that his stand-up act still wipes the floor with most of those who've come along behind him – indeed many of them have long given up the mental and physical demands of touring to settle for the more cosy life of the TV studio. Even in his 60s, Connolly's stand-up routines see him railing against authority, the press, the vacuous nature of latterday weather men, modern fire engines, Postman Pat and the

INTRODUCTION

solar system. Who else from the last 30 years of British comedy could you ever imagine having it in for the solar system?

Connolly stand-up is basically a critique of the world around him, and he's built up quite a library of stories and observations over the past 30 years of doing stand-up. The material is delivered in a free-flowing style that jumps around from subject to subject (as opposed to a series of gags with set-ups and punchlines); it isn't completely made up on the spot but as anyone who's seen him live will testify there's plenty of ad-libbing. Connolly himself has described the approach as having a skeleton of stories which he fleshes out on the night. "I've been intrigued since I was a wee boy by the way ordinary people behave," he's said. The result is a soup made from the bones of the core stories, things that might have happened that day or week, reaction to events within the auditorium such as someone getting up to go to the loo, or simply whatever Connolly-experience pops into his head. In an interview for *BBC Radio South Yorkshire* in 2003, Connolly acknowledged that one of his favourite descriptions had been in a Washington newspaper that said: "Connolly comes on stage with a Christmas tree and decorates it

INTRODUCTION

before your very eyes." With no live material ever written down it's a high risk strategy. What happens if he just dries up? Well, for Connolly the best way is often to rhetorically ask what he was talking about to jog his own memory, sometimes even getting a prompt from a member of the audience. Their ability to get involved in the performance and the danger inherent in Connolly's vulnerability help build a bond between Connolly and his audience – somehow there's a feeling during a Connolly show that everyone's in it together. But what appeals most of all is much more basic than that: the audience can identify with what Connolly's talking about because it's just his honest observations about the world around him, and everyone else. It's observational comedy in its purest form and the reason why he's so loved by audiences around the world.

Recent years have seen Connolly increasingly make his peace with the press, or perhaps that should be the press making peace with Billy. Like any superstar, there's still plenty of interest in his life, but where once he was hassled by the press over his private life, he's now started to receive the recognition he deserves for his contribution to the entertainment industry and British popular

INTRODUCTION

culture. On the journey to acceptance he's been friends with royalty, enjoyed a long and healthy showbiz marriage and had stars of the magnitude Dustin Hoffman and Robin Williams singing his praises. He's been on *This Is Your Life* before he'd even lived it and had a 1992 *South Bank Show* devoted to him to mark 25 years in the business.

Another of his proudest moments came in 2003 when he received the CBE from the Prince of Wales, probably one of the only times that a celebrity has received an honour from someone who was a guest at his birthday party a year earlier. Billy joked that Prince Charles was "wearing his mother's dress" because he was filling in for the Queen. Only the late Spike Milligan had ever previously built enough mutual respect with the heir to the throne to risk such a joke, when he called Charles a "little grovelling bastard" (Charles led the tributes when Milligan died). Receiving honours at the same time as Connolly were other survivors from the great comedy milieu of the 1970s – a CBE for Richard Briers, an OBE for Bill Oddie and an MBE for *Carry On* star Jim Dale.

It may be because Connolly has always been turning his hand to something new that he appears younger than his 61 years and it seems

INTRODUCTION

odd to see him picking up awards of the "lifetime achievement" variety. By the time he went to the Palace for his gong, he'd already received the People's Award for Outstanding Contribution to the Arts, in 2002, beating off competition from Harry Potter creator JK Rowling. The important word to note in the title of that award is "arts". The accolades Billy receives are far more than being just a teller of funny stories. His film career is well into double figures and he's won over hard-to-please film critics with his acting ability, sometimes as the shining light in movies where the overall results have been disappointing. He's acted alongside the likes of Robert Redford and Richard Burton, played serious drama in the theatre, been in an opera, seen his famous big banana boots become a museum piece, had his own sitcom in the States, toured the world on a motor bike for TV, helped raise immeasurable amounts of dosh for good causes, been friends with royalty, played elephant polo with Ringo Starr, hosted a birthday tribute for Nelson Mandela and become one of the most recognisable faces of the late twentieth century. He's not just liked, he's loved by millions of fans who continue to pack out theatres wherever he's playing, and their affection for him

BILLY CONNOLLY

INTRODUCTION

is evident in the reaction to the book by his wife, Pamela Stephenson, that revealed an anguished childhood, a story told with his usual honesty. He's done it all with energy and colour (one of Billy's pet hates is "beige" people living "beige" lives, preferring to think of his own look as "windswept and interesting").

And all this from a former shipyard welder who spent the early years of his life living in a two-room apartment in a working class Glasgow tenement. As Michael Parkinson might say at this point, ladies and gentlemen, please welcome... Billy Connolly.

2

The early years

BILLY CONNOLLY

THE EARLY YEARS

T he Big Yin has always been big. Billy Connolly was born on 24 November 1942, weighing a whopping 11lb 4oz. Kitchens featured heavily in Billy's early life. He was born on the floor of one and until the age of three lived in a recess in the same room, one of two that comprised the family abode in a nineteenth century Glasgow sandstone tenement block at 65 Dover Street, in the Anderston area. Although far from the worst stock of working class housing in Glasgow at the time, Anderston was on the way to being what would be regarded as a slum once the war was over. There was no bathroom, just a communal toilet, and if you

THE EARLY YEARS

wanted a bath you had one (cold, naturally) in the kitchen sink.

Billy shared his alcove with his sister Florence, Connolly's senior by a year-and-a-half. The brown-eyed and blond-haired baby Connolly was born into a family that, like the rest of the world at the time, was being torn about by war. His father, William, was conscripted into the RAF as an engineer and would soon be off to the Far East. In peacetime, William senior had made optical instruments for the Glasgow company Brooks & Stroud's. It was while working there that the 21-year-old William had met Mary McLean, a lens polisher whose family hailed from the Isle of Mull. She was the only girl in a family of five children. Her father, Neil, worked on the Glasgow buses for 40 years. He was always immaculately turned out for work and a tough disciplinarian with his children. Flora, her mother, worked as a cleaner, but loved to dress up and let her hair down.

William was the youngest of six children born to Jack, an emigrant from Ireland in the Twenties, and Jane Connolly (née McLusky), a Glaswegian from a devout Catholic family.

William and Mamie (as Mary was known to

THE EARLY YEARS

the family) married at St Patrick's in Anderston on 25 November 1940, less than a year after they first met. Mamie was already pregnant with Florence who was born five months later.

Billy was born almost two years to the day after the wedding, and was christened at St Patrick's, the same church where his parents had married. The still-very-young Mamie found herself bringing up two children by herself with an absentee husband and father.

In one of Billy's earliest memories he recalls how Florence used to frighten him while they were in bed by reflecting the light from a mirror on to his face. Although this upset the infant Billy, Florence would soon become what he referred to in later life as his "guardian angel". Mamie's evidently found it difficult to cope. Billy had pneumonia three times before he was four and the tiny Florence would often be left to look after Billy on her own.

When William senior was demobbed he returned to Glasgow, but he found it hard to bond with his children and he never reconnected with Mamie. He worked long hours and was seldom at home. The couple separated in 1946. Mamie was just 23 when she walked out on Florence and Billy, then aged four, and moved to Dunoon, 30 miles

THE EARLY YEARS

away. Although Billy and his mother disputed the exact number or timing of occasions, it's clear Mamie saw little more of Billy during his childhood.

Billy and Florence were taken in by their aunts Mona and Margaret, William's sisters who shared a house with their uncle, James. William Connolly lived in the same house but the culture of the times meant that it was effectively the aunts who brought up the children.

Billy and Florence stayed on good terms with their maternal grandparents, Angus and Flora, a woman with a passion for boxing whom Billy adored. She'd often tell him "you're heads full of dabbities" whenever he was talking childish gibberish.

The aunts and children lived in a two-room tenement apartment in Partick. At first, Billy slept in a cot in his aunts' room and the children received more attention than they were accustomed to. But over time the aunts became resentful of having to bring up someone else's children, particularly as they were still young and wanted to have a good time and possibly have families of their own. When Billy was six, Mona had a son, Michael, born out of wedlock and doted on by his mother. Billy ended up sharing a sofa-bed with his father in the living

THE EARLY YEARS

room as space became cramped.

Billy has often talked about the lack of basic love in his childhood. He once told Michael Parkinson in an interview: "I'm deeply envious of it – people who got kisses from their parents and stuff. I was never kissed as a child." Indeed the first kiss he can remember came from Gracie McLintock, a girl handing them out to a group of boys when Connolly was six. He remembers it with affection to this day. But it was far more than a lack of love that was the problem. In a *South Bank Show* of 1992, the comic described his childhood as "deeply violent".

Billy's first school was the girls' section of St Peter's, a Catholic primary school. The newly starting bairns, of whichever sex, served an apprenticeship with the girls before the boys moved to the big boys' school when they were six. Billy was an early success. Florence had taught him to write and his ability to do so led to him being paraded around the school as a good example to others. But the strict regime soon began to take its toll and Connolly would quickly come to hate school, a feeling he couldn't shake off for the rest of an inauspicious academic career. He abandoned the idea of ever doing homework early

THE EARLY YEARS

on and often found it difficult to concentrate. Though clearly bright, he was prone to drift off into his own private reverie.

If the school regime was demotivating, there was little more encouragement on the home front. Mona especially used to say that he would never make anything of his life. Even school would be no escape as disciplining the pupils often took the form of beatings.

Billy proved resilient to the discipline at the time, but the verbal humiliation left him more scarred, and the put-downs expressed by others took root as a nagging self-doubt that has stayed with Connolly throughout his success-strewn career.

But he was still confident enough to feel good about himself when his own playground misfortunes brought laughter from other children. He enjoyed making his peers laugh, a discovery for which millions of fans around the world would become eternally grateful. He also formed his own gang, although in those days to do so meant being armed with a catapult and a good dollop of cheek rather than an unhealthy malevolence and a blade. As with all mischievous kids, there were relatively trivial encounters with the police, but they would normally be sorted out with the proverbial clip around the ear.

BILLY CONNOLLY

THE EARLY YEARS

Billy failed his 11-plus, the widely scorned exam which all children took to decide whether they went to a prestigious grammar school or a somewhat stigmatised secondary modern.

Billy's new school, St Gerard's, turned out to one of the more well regarded working class schools, with a better rapport between teachers and children. He still struggled academically but found the environment more helpful and tolerant. But Billy was still something of a dreamer and formed the view at a very young age that he was somehow different from other people. Of course, the conjunction of this and the way his career eventually turned out may be nothing more than coincidence, but it certainly meant he was confident, even while still at school, to go public with a desire to become a comedian. He confided as much in his science teacher Bill Sheridan, although neither of them had the faintest idea how to go about becoming one. Kids of the Fifties were nowhere near as savvy about the ins and outs of showbiz as they are today. Mr Sheridan remarked that Connolly's footballing ability suggested he already was a comic. Billy's self-awareness of his 'difference' would prove much more useful in guiding his future path in life than

THE EARLY YEARS

a bagful of good qualifications could have done, even if he had managed to achieve them. As it was, he left school with just two engineering certificates.

For the last couple of years at school, Billy faced a long bus ride to St Gerard's, as the extended family moved to Kinfaus Drive in Drumchapel, a stark estate some 10 miles away and which had no schools. The new flat had a separate bathroom and kitchen for the first time and Billy didn't have to share a bed with his father. Billy wasn't too keen on the place; although he later described it as being pleasant enough, it was a long way from anywhere a teenager thought worth going to, and it cost a lot to do so.

Like most teenagers, Billy started to take an interest in music, a passion that would influence his early show business career.

Rock 'n' roll was still fresh off the blocks and Billy snapped up singles by Little Richard, Chuck Berry and Jerry Lee Lewis from the nearest branch of Woolworth's to play on the gramophone at Kinfaus Drive.

The small luxuries of life became more affordable in Billy's last year at school when he got a job as a milkboy on a delivery round. It was his first step into the world of work that would help shape his comic routine in future years.

BILLY CONNOLLY

THE EARLY YEARS

But the freedom of being a wage-earner came at a price. While out on a round he slipped and injured his hand on some broken glass, requiring a tendon transplant that forced him to miss out on much of his later schooling. His later career obviously shows him as a man of intelligence beyond the level of two engineering certificates.

Billy eventually escaped the tyranny of childhood at the age of 15 when he took his first proper job as a book delivery boy for John Smith's, a bookseller in the centre of Glasgow. Despite his lack of application in the classroom, Billy had grown to love books while still at school, borrowing them from the library. William Golding's tale of warfare among schoolboys marooned on a desert island, *Lord of the Flies*, grabbed his attention, and his job now brought him into contact with the works of writers including Neville Shute and Robert Burns. But the position with Smith's was not to last long, as Billy became the innocent victim of a purge after a book theft scam was discovered within the company.

These were times of high employment when it was not difficult to find work and Billy was quickly back on the food delivery rounds, with a job as a van boy for Bisland's Bakers. While out on rounds or making his way home he would constantly see ships plying the Clyde and, dreamer that he was, imagine the exotic locations of the registrations cities stamped on their sides, such as Shanghai or Baltimore. He formed an idea that he would become an engineer in the shipping industry which would get him on board and off to visit these places. The engineering certificates would surely be the magic ticket.

Unfortunately for the 16-year-old, they proved good enough only to get him a place as an apprentice welder in the Govan shipyards. It was a start, but little could the young Billy Connolly have imagined at that time that he would end up seeing many of the exotic places he dreamed about in quite different circumstances from those he had planned. The colourful characters and quick wit of the shipyards would provide the essence of the lovably aggressive style of humour that the whole nation would eventually see. He was special – and his arrival in the shipyards was a big step on the road to proving it.

3

The breakthrough years

BILLY CONNOLLY

THE BREAKTHROUGH YEARS

The Clyde shipyards today are but a shadow of their former glory. Back in the Fifties, they were a significant force in shaping the city's culture and attitude. For a teenage boy with a weakness for daydreaming, the ships that sailed past offered the distant chance of escape that would otherwise not be available to working class people. After all, they were never going to join the ranks of, say, film stars or international recording artists with all the glamour of overseas travel that came with that lifestyle, were they?

The way to travel was to become a marine engineer which was Billy's original plan, but he actually ended up with a job as an apprentice welder in Stephen's Shipyard in 1958, aged 16, living at home and earning £20 a week, actually one of the better apprentice wages in the yards. This meant that wanderlust would not be immediately satisfied, although his welding experience did earn him a spell working on a Nigerian oil rig eight years later. The urge to travel would soon be satisfied when Billy joined the volunteer Territorial Army for a three-year tour of duty that took in Cyprus among other places. As well as jumping out of aeroplanes, he did impromptu singing performances in a Scottish pub and a Nicosia nightclub, encouraged by his TA buddies.

But his bread-and-butter was in the dry workshop on Clydeside, and although his feet were very much on dry land, it was the start of another journey that would inspire the content and the over-the-top style of storytelling that characterises Connolly's live act. The routines he became famous for were rarely about joke-telling in the traditional sense, more embellishments and elaborations of his own observations of the weirdness of human life. The humour of the shipyards was at once bleak and warm, cruel and affectionate, and Billy absorbed

THE BREAKTHROUGH YEARS

this pattern into his own stage persona.

It wasn't just the shipyards that inspired Connolly's routines. As anyone who's seen him perform live knows, his stand-up is peppered with comic characters and observations that come from places of work, the extended family and the school playground. Although Billy's father had made optical instruments for a living, like many Glasgow youngsters, the shipyards were in Connolly's blood. His grandfather, Jack, had worked in the yards. The shipyards were a place of wicked banter and wild practical joking and Billy soon became a part of this culture. At work, he was routinely called the Wee Yin, and although Billy eventually progressed to become the Big Yin in show business, the epithet is by no means unique to Connolly.

Away from work, recreation took Billy towards music and the dancehalls of Glasgow that were spinning the latest tunes from the likes of Bill Haley and Chuck Berry or putting on live bands performing Glaswegian versions of the hits of the day. In his earlier years, Billy had grown to love country music too, in particular Hank Williams. He had been enamoured of folk music programmes on TV, which convinced him that playing the banjo would be part of his future. He

THE BREAKTHROUGH YEARS

took his first lessons at the Glasgow Folk Centre and later approached Ron Duff, a banjo player he saw and admired on stage, for extra tuition to take him on to the next level. It was the first practical steps on the way to becoming a performer. It would be folk, rather than rock 'n' roll, that Billy came to be known for, and there was a parallel between the genre's songs about real people living real lives and the stories that eventually supplied his comic material.

The first group Billy was invited to join on the Glasgow folk circuit was the Tannahills, but soon Billy had formed his own band, the Skillet Lickers with Jim Carey and George McGovern. This was swiftly followed the Acme Brush Company, a very loose collective of players, with a semi-serious philosophy and practically a different line-up for every gig.

According to Connolly's own version of the legend, the between-song banter that was to signal a career in stand-up happened by chance. Billy was invited to do a solo gig supporting the folk singer Jimmy Steel in 1965. Performing the song *St Brendan's Isle*, Billy froze mid-song. Instead of trying to pick up where he left off, he started chatting to his audience about his gaffe and

THE BREAKTHROUGH YEARS

humming the tune. The audience loved his self-deprecating approach and were quickly on Billy's side. It was the first accidental outing of the Billy Connolly style of comedy and another pivotal moment in his career.

In the same year, Connolly formed the Humblebums with Tam Harvey, again playing folk songs in clubs and pubs across Scotland. One night he bumped into a young guy called Gerry Rafferty who offered his song-writing talents to the duo. Billy's initial reaction was sceptical about the newcomer's claims about his own prowess, but when he heard Rafferty's songs he was convinced. Harvey was eventually sidelined and Connolly and Rafferty continued using the Humblebums name. A recording contract saw them produce two albums that won both acclaim and sales in Scotland. When playing live, it was Billy's between-numbers patter that increasingly came to the fore. The Humblebums eventually split in 1970. As a solo artist, Rafferty went on to have three top 40 hits – ironically one less than the string of novelty hits enjoyed by Connolly – including *Baker Street*, widely acknowledged as a pop classic and containing one of the most famous

THE BREAKTHROUGH YEARS

sax solos of all time. His early Seventies group Stealer's Wheel released *Stuck in the Middle With You*, which became a worldwide hit many years later when used in Quentin Tarantino's film *Reservoir Dogs*.

By the time of the split, Billy had already decided his future lay away from the yards and that show business was going to be a full-time career. His inspiration came from a pep talk from an older co-worker in the yard, about his regret at not leaving when he was younger. Billy vowed not to make the same mistake.

By the end of the year, Billy was performing regularly as a solo artist. Although overly modest about his own musical abilities, Connolly was no slouch with a guitar or banjo in his hands, becoming an accomplished player. Word spread like wildfire about this strange bearded, strangely dressed singer who chatted about naughty subjects like sex and toilet habits between songs, leaving his audiences in stitches. It wasn't long before he was approached to do a regular song slot on a Scotland-only talk show called *Daytime*. This brought another huge leap forward in Billy's career, when a guest pulled out from the show one day and Billy was invited to

THE BREAKTHROUGH YEARS

fill in as a fully fledged interviewee. It was a performance that not only made his name in Scotland but at an early stage marked out chat shows as a territory that Billy could make his own. The king of British TV chat, Michael Parkinson, has since speculated that Connolly flourishes in that TV format because it's the only one that gives Billy's anarchic and ad hoc delivery a free reign.

In 1972, he wrote a sketch show with humourous songs thrown in, called *The Great Northern Welly Boot Show* for the Glasgow Mayfest, with the poet Tom Buchan. The reception was muted but when the show was revived for the 1973 Edinburgh fringe it became a success. A run at the Young Vic in London followed.

With a new manager on board in the shape of Frank Lynch, the Wee Yin was transforming into the Big Yin, in Scotland at least. However, he wasn't universally popular. A Glasgow pastor, Jack Glass, took issue with what he saw as the outrageous nature of some of Billy's material, particularly a version of the last supper and the crucifixion set in downtown Glasgow. Pastor Glass took to leading his followers in protests outside Billy's concerts, the start of a rivalry that

THE BREAKTHROUGH YEARS

would endure for many years to come.

A solo live album was released, reaching 18 in the national charts on the back of sales north of the border, but Billy Connolly was still little-known down south, and that was a situation that needed to be addressed if his career was to progress.

4

Bright lights, big city

BILLY CONNOLLY

BRIGHT LIGHTS, BIG CITY

T he bush telegraph proved to be more powerful than Billy imagined when Lynch booked the London Palladium to perform a live show on 12 January 1975. The show sold out on the strength of sales to ex-pat Scots. It was a feather-in-the-cap but still meant that the audience was primarily Scottish. A subsequent tour took in the north of England and Ireland. The Irish leg was filmed for a documentary called *Big Banana Feet*.

The Palladium show started a buzz in the capital, but there still wasn't anywhere near universal awareness of the long-bearded Glaswegian with a propensity to wear leotards

with boots in the shape of half-peeled bananas on
stage. That was all to change with a chance
conversation between Michael Parkinson and a
Glasgow cabbie.

A thin and gangly Billy Connolly, dressed in
a leather suit the colour of a Caramac bar, strides
on to the set of Parkinson and immediately looks
confident and at home next to the chat show host.
In the Seventies and early Eighties, Parkinson
was part of an institution of BBC Saturday night
broadcasting that included family favourites such
as *The Two Ronnies*, *The Generation Game* and
Yarwood. *Parkinson* was the late-night come-down
from the pub and/or *Match of the Day*. Many of its
shows have passed into legend: brassy young
football manager Brian Clough jousting with Don
Revie, the old duffer whose job he'd taken; Rod
Hull's Emu wrestling Michael Parkinson and a
coffee table to the floor; numerous appearances in
which the boxing legend Muhammad Ali seduced
the British public with his eloquence, good looks
and charisma.

Parkinson would later go on record as
saying that only two guests from that era were
guaranteed to put two million on the viewing
figures. Ali was one, and the other was Billy

BILLY CONNOLLY

BRIGHT LIGHTS, BIG CITY

Connolly. The occasion of the Caramac-coloured suit was Connelly's first appearance on national TV and the moment when he stopped being a Scottish oddity and was catapulted into stardom across Britain. The following Monday morning, Connolly's performance was the talk of offices and factory floors across the nation. Its success hinged on the risky and risqué telling of a joke with an identifiable punchline, something which would oddly never become a Connolly stand-up trademark. Connolly had been told the joke a few days before and his manager Frank Lynch was mortified at the idea that Connolly would repeat it on live TV. The joke, which concerned a man using his dead wife's backside to park his bike in, may be familiar in various forms today and considered rather tame, but back in 1975 it was both dangerous and funny enough to put Connolly on the show business map.

Parkinson had been alerted to Connolly by a Glasgow cabbie who'd insisted he was a must-have guest for the show and put a copy of one of his LPs into the chat show host's hands. After that first magical encounter, Billy would be asked back by Parkinson again and again in the years to follow and the chat show host became arguably his most loyal fan – and eventually a close friend. Parky's introductions would usually refer to Connolly as one of *the* funniest men on the planet, if not the funniest in the view of one of the era's most popular broadcasters. Even on that first appearance, Parkinson was already well on his way to being a member of the Billy Connolly fan club, describing him as "one of the most original and best comedians I've heard for many a day". Connolly himself acknowledged that the programme changed his life forever. Scottish critics had worried that English audiences would fail to take to Connolly's belligerent style of Glasgow comedy and broad accent. How wrong they were.

But Connolly was still only halfway to becoming the full-on stand-up comedian that would be his stock-in-trade for the next decade. Music was still a big part of the act, albeit that the serious folk music was giving way to self-penned humourous ditties and parodies of hits of the day.

In the April 1975, the US country star Tammy Wynette scored her first British hit, when *Stand By Your Man* went to number one for three weeks. Two months later, she was back in the charts with *D.I.V.O.R.C.E.* It too was a hit, but only made it as high as number 12. In the autumn, a Polydor records executive suggested it would be a good one for Billy to cover, but of course instead of doing it straight, he put his own twist on it by adding moderately naughty words and turning it into a three-minute comic cameo. The besotted British public loved it and the record went to the top of the charts for a week in November 1975, between stints for David Bowie's re-released *Space Oddity* and Queen's *Bohemian Rhapsody*, which was on its first orbit round the pop galaxy.

By the time Billy came to play in London again, it was to packed houses and it wasn't long before there were hints at the future acting career that would become a big feature of Connolly's life, as he was approached to appear in a brace of TV dramas, first in *Just Another Saturday* and then in *The Elephant's Graveyard*. Although only playing supporting roles in each, there was evidence that Connolly was as natural playing serious roles to a camera as he was playing the fool to a live audience.

Billy was also still toying with comedy versions of pop hits of the time, but their effect was cooling as the public instead warmed to the storytelling and wicked line in observation that was his stand-up routine. In 1976, a version of JJ Barrie's execrable spoken-word number one *No Charge*, reworked by Billy as *No Chance* made a respectable but unspectacular number 24. Three years later he was still at it, with the eminently more memorable *In the Brownies*, a send up of the Village People's pop-disco classic *In The Navy*. In the video Billy appeared playing four parts, all in Brownie costume, but wearing the headgear of the Village People characters. Although it stayed in the top 75 for seven weeks, it never got higher than number 38.

Also in 1976, Billy touched the real pop world when Elton John invited him to support his US tour. Audience reactions were mixed though largely favourable, but it was some years before Connolly would find the key to fame Stateside. A three-week tour of Australia under his own steam in 1977 was blighted by a hostile crowd in Brisbane, although audiences elsewhere in the country loved him, as they did on a lengthy 50-plus night slog around the UK.

Over the next couple of years there was more touring but Billy found time to write and put on three plays, *An' Me Wi' Me Bad Leg Tae, Groan Up* and *When Hair Was Long And Time Was Short.* They first appeared at the Edinburgh Festival and went on to the Royal Court in London.

Up seemed to be the only way, and in 1979, Billy was pencilled in to appear on *This Is Your Life.* Like *Parkinson, This is Your Life* was a TV institution in the Seventies. Unlike today, there was a tendency to keep the subjects identity a secret until the day of screening which gave the show an extra frisson that's arguably missing today. And an appearance really seemed to say that you'd made it, even if the detail of the programme making didn't always live up to the billing. Billy was famously presented with an encounter with an old shipyard colleague, who sure enough had the right surname but who Billy had never set eyes on before. Elton John was among the more familiar faces there to sing Billy's praises.

In the same year, Billy was invited on to the cult BBC2 comedy *Not the Nine O'Clock News.* He played himself in a sketch opposite a young Australian actress called Pamela Stephenson and his life was about to turn another corner.

BILLY CONNOLLY

BRIGHT LIGHTS, BIG CITY

Spotlight on... Billy and Parky

It was on Michael Parkinson's BBC1 chat show that Billy Connolly first came to prominence south of the border. Since that time Connolly has appeared on the show again, and again, and again. When the first run of the popular Saturday show ended in 1982, Connolly was one of the last guests. Billy and Parky remained good friends with Parky turning up at Connolly's shows.

In Connolly's drinking days, the two would often enjoy a drink together, and they were as pally off-screen as on-screen. On one alcohol-aided occasion they danced together in the middle of the traffic in the busy King's Cross area of London before fleeing the approaching police.

Connolly's drinking stopped. In 1998, Parky returned to his old Saturday night slot and within a couple of weeks he was joined by his old TV sparring partner. As before, he hardly needed to ask a question to get the flow of fresh anecdotes coming. In fact, before long, amid tears of laughter, Parky stopped trying altogether and simply sat back to enjoy the company of an old friend.

Connolly was to return to the show again, alongside Sting in late 1999 which gave him the

BRIGHT LIGHTS, BIG CITY

opportunity to join in with the former Police frontman to add to the musical flavour of the show. He then appeared with his wife Pamela in October 2001 when he revealed what it was like living with your biographer.

Parkinson finished its long run on BBC1 in spring 2004 with the show's host deciding that he didn't want to host an early Saturday night programme now that Match of the Day is to take his favourite post-10pm slot. Instead, Parky has decided to jump channels and head for ITV1.

It shouldn't be too long before Parky is joined for a chat by a certain bearded Scottish friend.

5

Pamela Stephenson

BILLY CONNOLLY

PAMELA STEPHENSON

When *Not the Nine O'Clock News* first appeared on BBC2 for a six-week run in 1979, it quickly became a comedy must-see for those in the know, and then shortly after a national phenomenon. Cheekily given a time slot alongside BBC1's real *Nine O'Clock News* (in those days the BBC was rigidly fixed to 9pm and ITN to 10pm for their late evening bulletins), the set-up of the comedy show was simple: a series of sketches with a political, satirical edge, not frightened to stretch the sensibilities of its viewing public, and, above all, wildly funny. Britain was still recovering from the shock of

PAMELA STEPHENSON

punk, and that movement's DIY spirit could be found in the way the soundtracks of sketches were allowed to overlap, and real news footage was woven into free-flowing comic sequences.

The programme was a showcase for new comic talent. The world first got to see Rowan Atkinson's range of malleable facial expressions. Mel Smith tended to play "outraged of Tunbridge Wells" types. Griff Rhys Jones' cheesy grin landed him cheeky rogue parts, and Pamela Stephenson took female roles. Atkinson would go on to Hollywood via *Mr Bean* and *Blackadder*. Smith and Jones would go on to forge a successful comedy partnership of their own. And Stephenson would eventually give up comedy to become a clinical psychologist – and would marry Billy Connolly.

Pamela and Billy's first encounter was a pre-production meeting for a *Not the Nine O'Clock News* sketch. The sketch was typical of the style of the programme as it was both brief to fit in with the show's fast-flowing style and extremely silly. Billy's role was just to be himself, and, perhaps appropriately, it was in the role of "Billy the chat show guest" for which he was then most famous. The purpose of the sketch was little more than to poke fun at the broadcaster Janet Street Porter,

PAMELA STEPHENSON

played by Stephenson in the role of chat show host. The show was a great vehicle for Stephenson's masterful mimicry: each episode had a core spoof news bulletin interspersed between sketches, anchored by Smith and Stephenson. Mel played his role straight down the line, but Stephenson aped the exaggerated delivery of BBC1 newsreader Angela Rippon, particularly her overly precise pronunciations of foreign dignitaries. She was so good that the audience never needed to be told who she was meant to be.

The show spawned book and record spin-offs and was at the forefront of the movement that would become known as "alternative comedy" and would spawn such shows as *The Comic Strip Presents* and *The Young Ones* in the early Eighties and give the world stars such as Ade Edmondsen and Rik Mayall. But Billy Connolly was already ahead of the game. In a BBC retrospective on Connolly's career some years later, the comedian Eddie Izzard would observe that Connolly "was doing alternative comedy before anyone was doing alternative comedy". It's hard to imagine now that sex shops, and venere-al disease were once considered unsuitable comic material, even though tasteless jokes about

BILLY CONNOLLY

PAMELA STEPHENSON

mothers-in-law or "the wife" were. But a typical Connolly routine had him taking a blow-up doll back to a sex shop and complaining that "the first time I blow it up it goes down on me," to which the shopkeeper replies "if I'd have known that, I'd have charged you another fiver."

As well as the subject matter, Connolly's wild dress sense was somewhat out of the ordinary against the tuxedos and bow ties of the day. Here was a beige-hating, cussing Glaswegian with long hair and a beard ("the longest designer stubble in history") wearing banana boots, cowboy jackets and leotards. With the benefit of hindsight, Connolly's anarchic style made his involvement in a show that was consciously alternative seem entirely appropriate, but at the time he was already a big-name-guest for the fledgling programme.

In the Connolly sketch, Pam wore comedy teeth and huge spectacles in a parody of Street Porter and got her rolling cockney drawl spot on as she opened with: "Well hello, I'm talking to Billy Connolly, a well-known Scottish comedian. Billy, I understand that when you first came to England, people had a lot of trouble understanding your accent. Is that right?". Billy's deadpan punchline

PAMELA STEPHENSON

was simply, "sorry?", said with a troubled expression that broke into a stifled laugh before the characteristic cut to the next scene.

A convenient leap forward here would say that the couple fell in love and were soon walking up the aisle, but life's more complex than that and it would be another decade before Billy and Pamela's wedding in Fiji. Back in 1979, Billy was already married. He had been introduced to Iris Pressagh, an interior designer, in 1965 through friends on the folk circuit. When they married in June 1969, with Gerry Rafferty as best man, Iris was already pregnant with their first child, and James (or Jamie) was born in December of the same year. They first lived in pleasant areas of Glasgow's West End, but once Billy started to achieve a level of stardom, in Scotland at least, the home became a target for well-meaning but intrusive fans. The couple decamped to Drymen, a rural town which would become home through the years of Billy's national rise to fame. The couple's second child, Cara, was born in 1973 and was dubbed the sleepy dumpling by Connolly, a name he would later give to his own publishing company.

By the end of the Seventies, Billy's career

PAMELA STEPHENSON

had well and truly taken off and his national standing meant spending more time touring Britain, as opposed to Scotland, and more time, therefore, away from home. The 1979 tour took in 62 gigs, all of which were played to full houses. This included a straight run of six nights in the capital. In interviews, Connolly was talking of moving to London and the following year saw another mammoth tour of over 80 dates as demand for his live act seemed insatiable. In 1981, the tour focus shifted to Australia and New Zealand with a Middle Eastern sojourn thrown in for good measure. All this time away understandably put a strain on the marriage, as it would with anyone.

Pamlea Stephenson was married too, to the actor Nicholas Ball, a famous face as the star of TV detective series *Hazell*, a show famously co-written by future England soccer manager Terry Venables. She was a New Zealander, raised in Australia, and better-known as a straight actress down under before moving to Britain and the success of *Not The Nine O'Clock News*. It was a year after Connolly and Stephenson had first worked on *Not The Nine O'Clock News* before Billy and Pamela met again when she attended a live

PAMELA STEPHENSON

show in Brighton. Over the following months it gradually emerged in the press that Connolly and Stephenson had struck up a friendship, although talk of this being a relationship remained unconfirmed and the subject of press gossip. Both appeared in *The Secret Policeman's Other Ball*, a charity mix of rock musical and comedy at a London theatre. To avoid being photographed together, Stephenson left with the guitarist Eric Clapton, and Billy followed soon after.

Billy and Iris announced they were parting in separate announcements to the press in 1981 and Billy quickly indicated that he would not contest a divorce. Both blamed the conflicting pressures of Billy's show business career with family life in Scotland. The divorce may have been uncontested when it was confirmed in 1985, but that hadn't prevented a custody battle over Jamie and Cara which Billy won in the summer of 1983.

Billy and Pamela bought a house in Bray near Windsor, home of the wealthy and famous, although they sold it within three years because its riverside location meant they were snooped on by over-eager members of the public. Instead they bought a more secluded mansion in Windsor which they gave the name Grunt Futtock Hall, in honour of a Kenneth Williams character in the Sixties' radio show *Round the Horne*.

The couple's first child, Daisy, was born in 1983 when Billy's children from his first marriage, Jamie and Cara, were 11 and eight. Daisy was followed by another daughter for Billy and Pamela, Amy, born in 1986, and a third, Scarlett, in 1988. All three were bridesmaids when their mother and father eventually tied the knot in the exotic location of Fiji (where Pamela's grandmother had once lived) on 20 December 1989. The guests were summoned by invitations in the form of specially made sarongs. The music chosen for the occasion included the theme from radio soap *The Archers*, whose familiar and sprightly "dum-de-dum-de-dum-de-dum" refrain was a part of Connolly's live routine as a suggested alternative to the dreary *God Save the Queen* for the British national anthem.

Lest anyone should think Connolly's dislike of the national anthem represented a nationalistic Scotsman's disrespect for the Royal Family, nothing could be further from the truth. He was merely making an aesthetic off-the-wall judgment on the tune's qualities. In the 1985 *An Audience with Billy Connolly* TV special, the Big Yin joked that at major sporting events "the other nations

PAMELA STEPHENSON

never want us to win because it takes half an hour for the flag to go up the pole". One of Billy's most endearing qualities is his openness towards people from all backgrounds. He has the ability to feel equally at home with the poor and oppressed as the rich and powerful – he truly does appear to just take people as he finds them. Prince Andrew and Sarah Ferguson (later the Duke and Duchess of York) would become close friends with Pamela and Billy, much to both the delight and disgust of sections of the press.

Ever since Billy and Pamela had met, their relationship had been under the close scrutiny of the press. Although Pamela would soon take the unusual and admirable step of giving up her own show business career to retrain as a psychotherapist, they were and remain very much a showbiz couple. Connolly is full of praise for the way Stephenson switched to a career that relies on a candid but confidential relationship with clients. "She has turned her career around in a far more dramatic way [than himself]," he told *Saga* magazine in 2003. "She loves every second if it and is awfully good." In the same year he told the *Scotsman* newspaper: "My wife impresses the hell out of me. I'm more of an animal and she's more of a learned person. But I like being this and I admire that in her. We make two halves of one thing. I'm not sure what it is, but it's good."

Back in the Eighties, Connolly had to put up with repeated digs from the Scottish press about matters like his move south and his celebrity lifestyle. Run-ins with reporters and photographers had become a feature of the public Connolly persona in the early years of his fame. He'd even written a song about it: *You Take My Photograph (I Take Your Face)* which appeared on the LP *A Change Is As Good As Arrest*. Sample lyric: "In the darkroom I am going to get you and your camera/I know a trick and you are bound to love it/when I tell you where I'm going to shove it." After his divorce from Iris and subsequent marriage to Pamela, the press would have to find something else to gossip about. It wouldn't take them very long and when they did Connolly was on the verge of becoming an even bigger target – because the Big Yin was about to become an international superstar.

BILLY CONNOLLY

PAMELA STEPHENSON

Spotlight on... Billy's famous friends

In the fickle world of entertainment acquaintances are ten a penny, but behind the wide smiles and over effusive greetings there is rarely any great substance. In show business, the stars know how to put on a show – even if it's a show of affection for the cameras.

In the case of Billy Connolly, you get the strong sense that this is not the case. Other celebrities love being in his company and he genuinely enjoys being in theirs.

Michael Parkinson visibly brightens whenever Connolly walks onto the set. In the early Nineties Billy hosted the US broadcast element of the annual BAFTA ceremony. Every time the main British-based event crossed over to the States for Connolly to introduce the parts of the show where Hollywood-based stars who could not be in Britain received their awards, the viewer would be forgiven for thinking that the invited guests in Hollywood were enjoying a better show than the people at the main event. This was thanks entirely to the fact that Connolly is such good company and effortlessly adept at keeping any crowd happy – be they loyal fans in Glasgow or stellar Hollywood legends.

BILLY CONNOLLY

PAMELA STEPHENSON

Years earlier, when he'd been the star of *An Audience With*, it was clear that the vast majority of the celebrities in the audience were there to enjoy the buzz of a Billy Connolly performance rather than to get their faces on screen. Whenever a celebrity was called upon to ask Connolly a question, they asked something that they genuinely wanted an answer to from someone they respected.

He may always be keen (and able) to put on a good show himself, but he is just as willing to be entertained by other comedians – people he sees more as colleagues rather than rivals. This was witnessed by a privileged few in the foyer bar of the St Regis Hotel, Aspen, Colorado in late winter 2000. Each year, the American ski resort hosts a comedy festival. That year, Jerry Lewis was there to receive recognition for a lifetime's work, the voice cast of *The Simpsons* were there to perform classic episodes from the show live on stage and the cream of the American stand-up circuit were there to perform before their peers, journalists, TV executives and a small number of comedy fans lucky enough to get tickets for each event.

One afternoon in the middle of the 2000 festival, Robin Williams was being interviewed by a radio host in the St Regis hotel foyer. Williams was

PAMELA STEPHENSON

effortlessly entertaining the small crowd sat at a handful of tables in front of him. At one table sat Steve Martin, Eric Idle and Connolly. Williams may have been entertaining everyone present, but by far the person he was having the most effect on was Connolly who could be heard hooting throughout the interview, doubled up with laughter and frequently wiping away tears of delight. This was clearly no act, rather the natural reaction of someone who delights in enjoying the ability of other comedians to make people laugh.

His lavish 60th birthday party required many of his guests to make the extra effort if they wanted to attend. Rather than hold it in London or Hollywood, he opted to hold it several months early to coincide with his annual month-long stay in the Scottish Highlands. If guests wanted to attend his party, they would have to head far north. A 250-strong crowd did make the effort, providing local bed and breakfast establishments with some much-appreciated extra custom. Among the guests were the Prince of Wales, Camilla Parker-Bowles and Andrew, the Duke of York (who, to be fair, didn't have to travel too far as they were all based at nearby Balmoral at the time – nor did they need to make use of the local B&Bs).

BILLY CONNOLLY

PAMELA STEPHENSON

Also attending were Steve Martin, Robin Williams, Sir Bob Geldof and, of course, Parky. For most of the guests, getting to Connolly's retreat was something of an inconvenience, but to do so to celebrate their friend Billy's landmark birthday was clearly worth it.

6

The USA

BILLY CONNOLLY

THE USA

Marriage to Pamela was a catalyst to some big changes in Billy's life. As with most working class men from Glasgow at the time, Connolly had always liked a drink, but that was all to change as he became teetotal. He also became a vegetarian, took up meditation and shunned smoking. Drunks and drinking culture remained a big part of the live act but Billy decided he didn't need to go there himself to observe those who did. He still tells a story about the time he was trapped in a phone box after one too many unable to find the way out, and even pushing the wall with the phone on to see if that worked. Even as the twenty-first century dawned, Billy was praising the wonders of Guinness on a trip to Dublin in his BBC programme *Billy Connolly's World Tour*, but shots of alcohol-free lager were clearly in shot when Connolly was filmed jamming with a folk band in a pub. In fact, his reformed drinking character even bought him an advertising and sponsorship contract, from Guinness, for their alcohol-free lager brand Kaliber. The brand supported dates at the Hammersmith Odeon in London and used Billy in an ad that mimicked a Wonderbra poster of the time. The original had featured an attractive model wearing the bra and the caption "Hello Boys". The Connolly version – an implied joke about brewer's droop – had him sipping a can of the drink with the wording changed to "Hello Girls".

And there were other big lifestyle changes on the way as the Big Yin sought to make his name in comedy. On home turf, Connolly was a phenomenon; he'd sold out six nights at the Royal Albert Hall in 1987, a venue usually reserved for progressive rock bands and the *Last Night of the Proms*, rather than three-hour comic monologues. But the desire to always do something new has been a recurring theme in Connolly's career, and at this point the

BILLY CONNOLLY

THE USA

USA was the main challenge. Connolly was the first British comedian to make a conscious assault on the American market, driven by the feeling that his career would somehow be incomplete if he didn't make it there. Although Billy had played live in the USA before, that wasn't really the quickest root to stardom for a comedian. The vastness of the country meant that playing one-off gigs in towns and cities was just a tiny blot on the cultural landscape, but if you wanted to fill in all the gaps you had to make it on television. The trouble was that the stage rather than television had always been Connolly's natural home ground. Michael Parkinson has since observed how TV executives have always struggled to find the right format for him. Connolly's own vehicles were mainly one-off specials such as *Billy Connolly in Concert* in 1978. There was also an appearance fielding questions from 80 Scottish youngsters on *Out of the Question*, a programme which was given a UK-wide airing in 1985 under the title *The Big Yin*. In it, Connolly talked about his schooldays, his parents and why rock drummers made rich husbands! But arguably Connolly's most memorable TV outings had been on other people's shows – *Parkinson*, *Not The Nine O'Clock News*,

THE USA

and cameo guests slots on the *Kenny Everett Television Show*. After that, arguably his best shot at TV in Britain had been *An Audience With Billy Connolly*, a one-hour special on Channel 4, which featured Billy doing stand-up, with the added twist that it was to an audience of invited celebrities. The chunky sweaters and flicked hair-dos of some of the guests make it feel like something of an Eighties' period piece today, as do some of the guests themselves: Olympic 100-metre champion Allan Wells, football manager Lawrie McMenemy and then Coronation Street star Chris "Our Brian" Quentin. More enduring members of the audience included Ringo Starr, Bill Wyman, Bob Hoskins, Chris Tarrant, Jimmy Tarbuck and, of course, Michael Parkinson. Billy himself was dressed in a zebra print smock and tight black trousers. After greeting the audience with the line "it's decidedly average to be here", he worked his way through all the usual themes: politicians ("don't vote, it only encourages them"); his early life ("I was bought up as a Catholic in Partick. It was OK – I've got A Level Guilt"); and the absurdity of the world around him (a sign he spotted in America saying "To The Braille School"). It also featured his now legendary

THE USA

routine about the peculiar labour-saving devices that appear in the small ads: a bag to put your dog in to stop hairs being spread around the house and a single big slipper to keep both feet warm at once. The physical side of his humour was also on display as he staggered around the stage burdened by the weight of an imaginary pair of incontinence pants. *An Audience With* was a simple format that seemed to work for other comics who did similar shows too, but it wasn't one that gave a performer a sustained run in front of a TV audience over several weeks. That would be needed if Connolly was to create a name for himself with the American public.

Head of the Class was a TV sitcom which began in the States in 1986. The show was set in a Manhattan high school where a teacher, Charlie Moore, played by Howard Hesseman, took it on himself to teach his gifted charges more about the values and skills required to deal with life rather than any bookish knowledge. Like all US sitcoms of the modern era, it was filmed and shown in long runs, giving an audience a long time to grow into the style of the show and the characters. America's a big country and the word about a hit show needs time to filter from coast to coast. After being spotted in a live performance special hosted by *The Colour Purple* star Whoopi Goldberg, Connolly was asked to film a pilot for another sitcom. The show never got off the ground, but the pilot was seen by the makers of *Head of the Class* which they were looking to give a new direction after four years on the air. Connolly was recruited to join the show in 1990, playing Billy MacGregor, a Glaswegian teacher, educated at Oxford, who continues Moore's quest to educate the students in the practical ways of the world. Connolly went down well both with the US public and the critics, but his late arrival in the series meant he fell victim to its inevitable wearout. In true US style, the show ran for dozens of episodes (113 in all), over five years – but it was axed after Connolly had been in it for just a year. *Head of the Class*'s British slot was 7.35pm on BBC2, which in those days meant a clash with the popular soap *EastEnders* at its most fashionable, so the show didn't really make its mark in the Big Yin's home market.

In America, Connolly's performances in the later shows were viewed as one of its best attributes. Connolly had clearly impressed the TV execs as well as the viewing public, because when *Head of the Class* was axed, Billy was asked to stay on in

THE USA

his role as MacGregor in a spin-off series, which was clearly a vehicle for him. The series was part of a package reported at the time to be the highest-paid ever for a British TV star working in America. In the style of the big international sitcom hit of the time *Roseanne* (named after its central character and star Roseanne Barr), the new show was eponymously-named, 'Billy'. MacGregor was this time seen teaching poetry in an evening class at a community college. The writing team included Dick Clement and Ian Le Frenais, British sitcom writers who had moved to the US. They were in a good position to write about the central storyline which sees MacGregor enter into a marriage of convenience with a student to gain a green card. The show didn't last long and again Connolly's performances were the highlight of a lame duck show. Only 13 episodes were made, an incredibly short run for a US sitcom, and when they were shown on British television two years later, it was with a late-night midweek slot that ensured the programme's obscurity. Billy's professional move to America meant a physical one as well. He lived at first in a house on Sunset Boulevard, before being joined by the whole family in a luxurious house in the Hollywood Hills. Psychedelic rock star

THE USA

Frank Zappa and pop artist David Hockney were among the neighbours. Although he would eventually buy a rolling country estate in the Scottish Highlands, America would remain home."I love America – it's a great place," Connolly said in a 2003 interview. "People laugh at me on the plane to America when I say I am going home."

Billy has long had a difficult relationship with the Scottish press and the move to America only reinforced their feelings that he was becoming removed from the people who had first made him famous. He was lazily accused of "selling-out". Connolly's own open-minded view was that you could be Scottish and like Scotland, but that didn't mean you had to hate the rest of the world at the same time. Relations between Billy and the Scottish press would become stretched in 1990, as the American adventure was taking off, when Billy's mother was sought out by a reporter and presented to the world as in the "dark-secret" style of the tabloids. Of course, Billy had always known his mother was in Dunoon and he'd even met her on a couple on occasions. Indeed in the intervening years he's been more than generous about the circumstances in which his mother left him and his

THE USA

sister all those years ago. Appearing on the BBC Radio 4 programme *Desert Island Discs* in 2002 he said: "I've never held it against her, never. I think I might have done the same. She was a teenager, Germans were bombing the town. My father was in India and we lived in a slum in Glasgow."

Even so, the 1990 press "revelations" were an unwelcome intrusion at the end of a difficult time for the family. Billy's father had had a stroke back in 1984 and in February 1988, he had a second one. He died on the last day of March. Mamie became ill with motor neurone disease in 1993 and died shortly afterwards. Billy attended the funeral.

With the show 'Billy' axed, Connolly's career took something of a rare lull for him. There were guest appearances in the US sitcom *Pearl* and *The Tracey Ullman Show* (a Brit who found more fame and fortune in the US than at home), but it was not long before it was taking off in an entirely new direction altogether.

7

Hitting the big screen

BILLY CONNOLLY

HITTING THE BIG SCREEN

Billy Connolly, face contorted with anger, grabs a reporter by the lapels and throws him against a wall. Connolly has had run-ins with the press before, angry about their prying into his private life. But this time it's different: it's nothing personal. Unusually, the Big Yin is wearing a kilt (when receiving his CBE in 2003 he claimed he'd only ever wear one in Scotland). Queen Victoria is somewhere in the vicinity, and the reporter is a fellow actor on the set of *Mrs Brown*. The movie will turn out to be the highlight of a film career that has spanned 20 movies, with still more to come.

BILLY CONNOLLY

HITTING THE BIG SCREEN

While TV helped Billy Connolly crack the American market, it was for his work in cinema that he would eventually become best-known Stateside. If there's anything that stands out about Billy Connolly's career, it's the sheer diversity of his work. Although he's the arch clown, strutting across the stage berating his latest hate-targets, Connolly's passions have also been channelled into a broad love of the arts. When he was still a kid, he'd take trips to the Kelvingrove Art Gallery in Glasgow with his sister Florence. One painting by the surrealist artist Salvador Dali, *Christ of St John of the Cross*, had particularly captured his imagination. His early forays into the world of show business had been through the medium of "serious music" even if he hadn't been able to resist unleashing his verbal repartee between songs. Later, even when he was becoming established as a comedian, Connolly was doing straight acting in TV dramas and had trodden the boards with the company of the Scottish Opera, so it was no shock that he should end up in the movies. What did take many by surprise was that his film career would eventually establish him as a serious actor of some skill and discipline.

*Connolly started performing as a solo artist in 1970.
Word soon spread about this strangely bearded, strangely dressed
singer who chatted about naughty subjects like sex and toilet
habits between songs, leaving his audience in stitches.*

Now in his 60s, Connolly has been in show business for 40 years and he's still touring.

Billy Connolly as John Brown appearing alongside Judi Dench as Queen Victoria in the acclaimed film 'Mrs Brown' (1997). The film is based on the true story of Queen Victoria finding emotional support from her gamekeeper, John Brown, after the death of her husband, Prince Albert. Connolly's performance earned him a Golden Globe nomination.

Pamela Stephenson and Billy Connolly married in Fiji in 1989. Pictured arriving for the BBC's 'An audience with Billy Connolly' in December 2002.

BILLY CONNOLLY

HITTING THE BIG SCREEN

Many comics have attempted to make the crossover into serious movie acting, but no British performer of the last 30 years has made the transition quite as successfully as Billy Connolly. Peter Sellers was in *The Goon Show* on British radio before going on to become a huge Hollywood star, but was always best-known for roles such as Inspector Clouseau that were a vehicle for his tomfoolery. Dudley Moore had a comedy sketch career in *Beyond the Fringe* and *Not Only But Also* in the Sixties, before establishing himself as half of one of Britain's most famous double acts with Peter Cook. But when Moore left Britain to embark on a Hollywood film career, his Tinseltown roles seldom rose above romantic comedy whimsy. What marks Connolly's film career from his fellow wisecrackers is that he was more often than not asked to play rough-and-tough hoodlums rather than cinematic versions of his existing comic persona. Presumably there was something about his forbidding presence and Glaswegian accent that attracted casting agents seeking to fill such roles. Arguably the closest he would come to a great comic film role was playing Billy Bones to Tim 'Rocky Horror Picture Show' Curry's Long John Silver in the 1996 Muppet version of *Treasure Island.*

Even while still forging a name for himself as a comic in the Seventies, Billy Connolly was taking on dramatic roles for TV and had written his own stage plays, so the signs of thespianism were always there. He'd also appeared as the jailer in a Scottish Opera performance of Johann Strauss's *Die Fledermaus.* The circumstances in which he was offered his first film role shone a spotlight on to the diverse range of pies in which Billy already had a finger. He was on his *Seaside Extravaganza Tour*, playing British seaside tours in the dead of winter, when the call came through about a part in *Absolution.* Made in 1978, Connolly played the hippie nemesis of a priest in a Catholic boys' school. Although it offered the chance to appear with Richard Burton towards the end of his career, it took three years for the film to be released in Britain and proved a slow start to a film career that would not really lift off the best part of a decade.

It was 1983 before the next call came, a cameo in *Bullshot*, a spoof action-movie loosely based on the Bulldog Drummond adventure stories. The film was directed by Dick Clement, who with writing partner Ian Le Frenais had

HITTING THE BIG SCREEN

created hit sitcoms like *Porridge* and *The Likely Lads* in the Sixties and Seventies. The pair had moved to LA to make their names in Hollywood, beating Connolly by some years. In *Bullshot*, Connolly plays Hawkeye McGillicuddy, a blind man who refuses to accept that his affliction was caused by the commanding officer he lionises. The film also featured Mel Smith from the *Not the Nine O'Clock News* team whose own career had moved in the direction of film and Nicholas Lyndhurst, otherwise known as Rodney of *Only Fools and Horses*. The same year saw Connolly play Androcles in a BBC TV version of George Bernard Shaw's *Androcles and the Lion*.

The next celluloid project was in *Water* for HandMade Films in 1984. HandMade was the film production company founded by former Beatle George Harrison in 1978, which had made its mark with *Monty Python's Life of Brian* and Python member Terry Gilliam's *Time Bandits*. It would go on to make the darkly classic comedy *Withnail and I* in 1987 before disappearing off the cinema radar. The screenplay was another Clement and Le Frenais project, but *Water* (intended as a satire on recent skirmishes involving the US in the Caribbean island of Grenada and Britain in the

HITTING THE BIG SCREEN

Falklands) proved to be one of HandMade's less notable moments. However, for Connolly it was a blast working with Michael Caine, who would become a close friend, and filming part of the movie in St Lucia. The British leg of filming wasn't quite as much fun, as Billy was involved in a car accident on the way to the location, causing a delay in the shoot while he recovered in hospital.

In *Water* Billy plays Delgado, the half-Scottish rebel leader of a two-man guerrilla group who helps the English governor (played by Caine) of a small, sleepy British colonial island in the East Caribbean that has been ignored by the British for many years but which suddenly becomes the subject of great interest when an abandoned oil well turns out to provide an abundant source of mineral water. Before long, everyone wants a piece of the action including the British, the French, the Americans and even the Cubans.

In this early film role, Connolly demonstrated that he had the ability to transfer his talent for comedy and timing to the big screen. Not only did he get to act alongside Caine but also Leonard Rossiter, Maureen Lipman and Fred Gwynne (who had played Herman Munster in *The Munsters* TV series). Significantly for the lifelong music lover, he

HITTING THE BIG SCREEN

got to sing on-screen backed by none other than the film's producer George Harrison and two of the former Beatle's good friends – fellow Beatle Ringo Starr, and Eric Clapton.

The film may not have been a big commercial success but it does still have its fans. It is hard for anyone who has seen the film to argue that Connolly does not put in a good performance.

It was 1990 before Connolly's next big movie project hit the screens. Filmed a year earlier, *The Big Man* was notable because it was the first time a role demanded that Billy shave his beard off and have a tidied-up haircut. As moods and roles have come and gone through the 1990s and beyond, we've become accustomed to seeing a clean-shaven Billy Connolly from time to time, but back then it was quite a shock. In *The Big Man*, Connolly plays Frankie, the hardnut manager of a bare-knuckle boxer, Danny Scoular, a Scottish ex-miner played by Liam Neeson. Joanne Whalley-Kilmer and Hugh Grant also star in the movie. *The Big Man* was the last in a sequence of films that didn't fare well at the box office or go down with the critics, but for whose contributions Connolly invariably received praise. All that was going to change with the next string of releases.

BILLY CONNOLLY

HITTING THE BIG SCREEN

Billy's US sitcom career had blossomed and he was suddenly a name and a face around Hollywood. The director Adrian Lyne asked Connolly to appear in *Indecent Proposal*, a movie about a tycoon, played by Robert Redford, who offers Woody Harrelson (who'd made his name in the sitcom *Cheers*) $1 million to sleep with his wife, played by the then hottest of hot properties, Demi Moore. Connolly's role was a small one, a cameo as an auctioneer, but the film was both critically well-received and big at the box office. It also caused a minor moral panic, with the media conducting an ethical debate around the film's central premise. If there's no such thing as bad publicity, then it wouldn't cause Connolly's career harm to be associated with it.

In the 1994 TV play *Down Among the Big Boys* by Peter McDougall, Billy was back to the tough guy roles, as a Glasgow hoodlum, a role written with every intention that Connolly would fill it. TV seemed to be the way forward for the moment, as Billy followed up with the lead role in the *Life and Crimes of Deacon Brodie*, a BBC costume drama about a respectable Edinburgh councillor in the eighteenth century, who was hanged for the crimes he committed as a

HITTING THE BIG SCREEN

transformed character by night. Brodie's real life was said to have inspired the story of *Dr Jekyll and Mr Hyde*. But the switch to small screen drama proved to be short-lived – a year late, along came *Mrs Brown*.

8

Mrs Brown

BILLY CONNOLLY

MRS BROWN

With a CV as broad and as long as Billy Connolly's, it's difficult to pick out a peak: it's entirely plausible that it's still to come. But if you were looking to choose one, it would be in 1997 when he landed a plum role opposite Dame Judi Dench in *Mrs Brown*. Bearing the tagline 'Queen Victoria, the world's most powerful woman. John Brown, a simple Scottish Highlander. Their extraordinary friendship transformed an Empire.' The film is the true story of Queen Victoria (Dench) finding emotional support from John Brown (Connolly), a gamekeeper on the Balmoral estate, after the death of her husband Prince Albert.

MRS BROWN

Whether the real-life relationship between Brown and the queen ever went beyond the strongly platonic has never been truly revealed, and the film didn't seek to either prove or disprove the salacious rumours. Instead, it concentrated on the strong empathic bond between the gamekeeper and the queen. The film shows how Brown doggedly became concerned with the welfare of a woman who represents an English system of class and values that he utterly disdains. Connolly was masterful in his part as the straight-talking, no-nonsense Brown, bringing vigour and passion to the role. But he also proved to be technically strong as a film actor, displaying the restraint needed to succeed within the confines of the camera lens. On stage, Connolly struts back and forth like a hungry cockerel searching for scraps of corn, but he proved that when faced with a camera he can easily adapt to the need for physical self-control. In *Mrs Brown* he displays a subtlety that few actors who have gone through years of training can muster, let alone someone who is a comedian turned thespian.

The critics were, and still are, almost universal in their praise for the film and the performance of its two main stars, although there was a tendency by some to concentrate on

MRS BROWN

Connolly's appearance in a skinny-dipping scene. Dustin Hoffman, these days a confirmed big Billy Connolly fan, wasn't the only one who thought that Connolly was unfortunate not to get an Oscar nomination to match the one given to Dame Judi for her portrayal of Queen Victoria. In a later BBC Connolly tribute show, Hoffman said: "Talent is talent. I saw *Mrs Brown* and thought it was one of the most exciting male performances I'd seen that year." Connolly's part in *Mrs Brown* did earn a Golden Globe nomination, however. Billy was able to repay the Hoffman compliment when – at Hoffman's request – he presented a special show organised by BAFTA to showcase Hoffman's career. In typical Connolly style, the comic defused any potential pomposity in the occasion. "We have stars here you've never heard of," he told Hollywood's glitterati. He performed a similar trick a year later when asked to present a BAFTA Fellowship to Sean Connery, "this man who used to be my friend but would not admit to being my father," he joked.

Mrs Brown was received with rapturous acclaim by audiences on both sides of the Atlantic too, and remains Billy's biggest box office hit. That it became such is even more remarkable when you

MRS BROWN

consider the film was originally proposed as a TV drama, called *Her Majesty Mrs Brown*. Billy would later speculate that if it had been written for the big screen in the first place, his pal Sean Connery would have been given the part. Luckily for Billy and his fans, he was given the chance to play opposite one of the great British actresses of all time. "I'm a kind of common sod and she's a grand lady of the theatre," Connolly told the US newspaper *Tulsa World* in the same year. "Putting us together was a stroke of genius."

Filming *Mrs Brown* allowed Billy to expand his cultural and artistic interests in other directions too. A ball scene in the film featured dancers from Ballet West as extras, and Billy was so impressed with their skill and commitment that he later agreed to become the company's patron, posing for pictures with some of its members, although resisting the temptation to don a tutu, perhaps surprisingly for someone who had once appeared on stage wearing a leotard. One of Billy's motivations for becoming involved was to make ballet more accessible to a wider spectrum of people.

Another film that came out in the same year as *Mrs Brown* couldn't have had a more contrast-

MRS BROWN

ing role for the Big Yin. In the British-Australian comedy *Paws*, Billy supplied the Glaswegian voice to a Jack Russell called PC, who had been artificially provided with the power of speech by his techy owner. The movie was obviously something of a slapstick family romp, but Billy took the role seriously enough to turn in what was widely regarded as a brilliant performance. Without the familiar face even appearing on screen, Connolly was again able to provide one of the highlights of a film project in which he was involved.

With the buzz around *Mrs Brown*, Billy's film career was moving into overdrive. Also out in 1997 was *Middleton's Changeling*, a poorly-received version of a Jacobean tragedy that featured rock singer Ian Dury in the lead role. A year later, Connolly was back on the big screen again, playing the roadie of an ageing rock band in *Still Crazy*. The band, called Strange Fruit, comprised a pre-*Love Actually* Bill Nighy, Stephen Rea, Jimmy Nail (who like Connolly had been to the top of the real charts, with *Ain't No Doubt* in 1992) and Timothy Spall. The cast also included Phil Daniels of *Quadrophenia* fame and children's TV presenter Zoe Ball, also trying that movie crossover thing but with considerably less success than Connolly.

MRS BROWN

Once again the screenplay was written by Dick Clement and Ian Le Frenais. There was more than a little of *This Is Spinal Tap* in the set-up, but it was strong enough in its own right to go down well with the critics.

Another comic role in 1998 was in *The Imposters*, a farce in the truest sense of the word, in which the Big Yin played a gay tennis player. Stanley Tucci directed and took one of the two lead roles as out-of-work actors in 1920s America who stowaway on a sea-going liner.

And the offers just kept on coming. A year on and Billy was back on screen again in Anthony Neilson's *The Debt Collector*, in which Billy was back to the hard-man role, as a loan shark turned sculptor called Dryden, who is hounded by a past-it cop who once put him away. The film was described as "stunning" by *Uncut* magazine. *The Boondock Saints* in 1999 saw Connolly on the same cast list as Willem Defoe in the tale of a couple of working-class Boston youths who embark on a vigilante mission against the Mob.

Then there was a brief interlude for the TV drama *Gentlemen's Relish* in which Connolly played an Edwardian photographer (alongside Sarah Lancashire, formerly Raquel in *Coronation*

Street) whose artistic portraits are misinterpreted as pornography.

In 2000's *An Everlasting Piece* Billy plays a hairpiece manufacturer who scalps people so he can use their hair in a comedy set in Eighties' Belfast. The film also starred Barry McEvoy (who wrote the script too), Brian F O'Byrne and ex-*Brookside* star Anna Friel. *Beautiful Joe*, released straight to video in the same year, was a romantic drama, most notable for the fact that Connolly got to play a bedroom scene with Sharon Stone. Connolly is a florist from Ireland, ripped-off by Stone's white-trash character.

One of the quirkier plot set-ups in which Connolly has been involved was 2001's *The Man Who Sued God*. Billy plays Steve, a fisherman who also happens to have once been a lawyer. Steve does exactly what it says on the film box after his boat is destroyed by lightning and the insurance company refuses to pay out because it is deemed an act of God. An Australian production offered a rare chance for Billy to play the leading role, receiving praise for his performance opposite Judy Davis as the film's crusading journalist type. The same year saw the release of *Gabriel And Me* in which Billy plays a switched-on angel who

MRS BROWN

befriends a working class Geordie boy, in a script written by *Billy Elliot* scribe Lee Hall, and based on his radio play *I Luv You Jimmy Spud*. Billy, as the Archangel Gabriel, trains Jimmy in the angelic skills, which are then put to the test when Jimmy's father is diagnosed with lung cancer.

Billy's next film outing was in *Timeline* in 2003, written by *Jurassic Park* author Michael Crichton and directed by *Lethal Weapon*'s Richard Donner. It's a time-travelling adventure flick in which the Big Yin is an archaeologist trapped in fourteenth century France, and the cast again includes Anna Friel. And 2003 also saw Connolly's biggest box office movie since *Mrs Brown*, in the form of *The Last Samurai*. Billy is Zebulon Grant who recruits Tom Cruise's ex-army officer Nathan Algren to go to nineteenth-century-Japan to put down an uprising. *The Last Samurai* was reviewed strongly and performed well at the box office, but a common theme among critics of all Connolly's films is how often he's rated as one of the best things in it. Connolly is no novelty rent-a-cameo, but an accomplished serious actor. The contrast is stark between the confines of the screen and the wide open spaces of one man on the Hammersmith Odeon stage, but it's one in which Connolly revels.

MRS BROWN

"I like my boundaries. I really like the discipline of other people depending on what I do next," he told the *Scotsman* in 2003.

But don't expect Connolly to step out from behind the camera and take the director's chair: he remains a performer at heart. Promoting *The Last Samurai*, he said: "It's the doing of it that I like and the business aspect of it. I don't know anything about it and have no desire – never wanted to be a director."

Connolly's film roles took his career on to a plain that no other British funny man has ever reached, but there was still a public craving to see Connolly in their living rooms. A strong TV series had always eluded Connolly in Britain, but the Nineties finally saw that particular ghost laid to rest.

MRS BROWN

Spotlight on... the Laird of Cardacraig

In 1998, Connolly and his wife bought the estate and manor house of Cardacraig near Strathdon in the Scottish Highlands from Anita Roddick, the founder of the global Body Shop empire. They'd been attracted to the 15-bedroom house during the filming of *Mrs Brown* when Connolly had spent an extensive amount of time in the area in which the great house sits. Since then the new 'laird' has spent each August enjoying his Highland retreat and making the most of brief but beautiful Scottish summers.

In recognition of his commitment to the region, he has been made an honourary member of the Lonarch Society. Such an honour is rarely bestowed on an outsider and means that he can march with the Men of Lonarch each year at the start of the Lonarch Highland gathering. Although he tends not to march, he does invite them up to his house to enjoy a wee dram of whisky at the end of the march each year.

His involvement with the area has been more than symbolic. He donated the proceeds of a concert in Aberdeen towards the repair of the local Village Hall roof. At the gatherings, which involve

MRS BROWN

the playing of highly competitive traditional Highland games, he takes an active part in the proceedings and has roped in many famous faces along the way. In 2001, guests at the 160th gathering accompanying Connolly included former Python Eric Idle and Scottish actor and Star Wars star Ewan McGregor as well as Hollywood stars Steve Buscemi, Aidan Quinn and Robin Williams.

It's been reported in the local press that as many spectators now come to the event to catch a glimpse of Connolly and his famous friends as to watch the competitors. The organisers do not seem to mind too much, realising that anything that attracts more visitors is good for the continued success of the gathering. They said that everyone is welcome to be a spectator at the games – even if they were rich, famous and a distracting influence.

9

On yer bike

BILLY CONNOLLY

ON YER BIKE

Every nation has its blinkered types who think the world begins and ends at passport control. Billy Connolly was thankfully never one of those people. He has long been irked by the lazy assertions of some of his country folk that by moving first south to London and then abroad to America, he has abandoned his working class Glasgow roots. Those making the allegations might ponder for a minute what would have happened if Billy's paternal ancestors had themselves never left Ireland to seek work in Scotland; the Big Yin might never have been.

Billy's spirit of adventure and longing to see

countries other than his own had been with him since he was a boy watching the ships sailing down the Clyde and off to far-away places. It was evident again when, 40 years later, he set off on another "world tour" for British TV. The notion of the world tour was a play on words. The set-up for each series of programmes was that Connolly would embark on a "world tour" of a particular country, kicking off with his native Scotland. It was natural that he should start with the place that he knew best, and Australia, as a country he loved, as well as being the childhood home of his wife, was a natural choice for the second series. England, Wales and Ireland would be pushed together into a single package.

As a taster for the world tours, Billy spent a week living on an island off the coast of Greenland for a BBC documentary *A Scot in the Arctic*. The actress Joanna Lumley had already been packed off on an exotic video-diary-type shoot, but the Connolly trip to the cold wilderness where he ran the risk of being attacked by polar bears arguably took the format to a new compelling level. The video diary format had not then been done ad nauseum, so it was a novel experience for the British public to see one of its loudest and most

ON YER BIKE

confident comedy stars living a solitary existence on an iceberg with only occasional visits from the indigenous Inuit people and a camera crew for company. It was perhaps even more of a surprise to see that, far from becoming despondent with his solitary confinement, Connolly seemed almost to revel in the experience.

A Scot in the Arctic was a treat for Connolly fans who had been starved of his presence on the small screen during the onset of his movie career and his sojourn to the States. The start of the *World Tour* series would see Connolly return to being a fixture on British TV screens. The idea was that Billy would act as tour guide around some of his favourite places in the world, telling stories about their history, meeting some of the people who lived there, admiring the scenery and sampling the local culture and customs. In addition, he'd perform live shows, during which he'd recount anecdotes from his earlier encounters. The documentary and live performance footage were then spliced together to create a cohesive half-hour show. The idea of Billy talking about people he'd met that day wasn't created especially for the programme, but had been characteristic of Connolly's live performances throughout his career.

BILLY CONNOLLY

ON YER BIKE

All the elements put together resulted in a compact and comforting half-hour that was equal parts travel show, comedy and social history – the format that TV and Connolly had always been searching for in each other but never found. A common theme in the shows was Billy's passion for meeting new people, being pleasantly surprised by a twist of events or seduced again by familiar haunting grounds. An extra wee hook was that Billy would travel between venues either astride his beloved brute of a three-wheel Harley Davidson or behind the wheel of a bright yellow Land Rover, towing the bike behind.

Connolly's love affair with motorbikes began when he was still an apprentice welder and continued when he travelled between gigs on one for his suitably titled *On Yer Bike* tour in 1980. When he celebrated his 60th birthday with 200 guests at his retreat in the Highlands, a five-foot-high ice sculpture of the World Tour Harley was the centrepiece. (He's also an enthusiastic cyclist of the pedal variety and has successfully completed the London to Brighton run.)

The shows put Billy Connolly back into the public consciousness in his own country and – in the documentary footage at any rate – portrayed a

ON YER BIKE

more ruminative and languid Connolly than the public had previously seen. Scottish viewers had already had a sneak preview of this side of Billy when he presented a series on Scottish art called *The Bigger Picture*. But although the World Tour concert footage showed a slightly more restrained version of Billy Connolly, the old firebrand was far from dead, even if the dress code was ever so slightly more sober – usually a garish pair of trousers with a plain black T-shirt. He was still a robust performer with a keen eye and ear for the ridiculous, and unafraid to pull punches when necessary. Since those very early days when Connolly was a bona fide pop star as well as comedian, the music had taken more of a back seat in the live act: Connolly joked in the BBC retrospective *Erect for 30 Years* that he had a voice like "a goose farting in the fog". But Connolly's love of music was evident throughout the series: the programmes on Ireland featured jamming with a folk group in a Dublin pub, and the folk-tinged soundtrack was a key factor in the overall atmosphere of the shows.

The first eight-part series was the *World Tour of Scotland* in 1994, and included Billy ruminating on his love of the River Clyde, dancing naked round a stone circle and reciting poetry. It won Best Entertainment Programme at the Scottish version of the BAFTAs, and, as if to emphasise Connolly's versatility, *The Bigger Picture* took the prize for Best Arts Programme at the same time.

The public response was so positive that the *World Tour of Australia*, again in eight parts, followed in 1996 and attracted very respectable viewing figures of nine million. Filmed over 10 weeks, the vastness of the country inevitably required forms of transport other than the bike, but the Harley still put in an appearance, and the feel of a documentary road movie remained. The highlights included scaling the Sydney Harbour Bridge which Connolly, with his love of great works of industry considered "one of the wonders of the world". He remembered the time he took close-up photographs of the underside of the bridge, followed by similar shots of the Sahara Desert and the Empire State Building. When he later showed them to his father "the poor bugger thought I was off my head". In Australia, Connolly also visited the penal colony that had once housed the Scot Charlie Anderson, a figure who gained notoriety for his habit of swearing and cussing at

ON YER BIKE

passing ships, which prompted Connolly to suggest that he might record an appropriate soundtrack that could be played through loudspeakers on the same spot where Anderson had sat. And there was a trip to Botany Bay and Connolly's assertion that the Aborigines would have mistaken Captain Cook's use of the telescope for an abject attempt to play the digeridoo.

After the *World Tour of Australia*, Billy's film career moved into overdrive, especially with the release of *Mrs Brown* the following year. So it was six years before the idea was revisited with Billy Connolly's *World Tour of England, Ireland and Wales*. To plug the gap, the BBC screened a stand-up half-hour special, *Billy Connolly's One Night Stand* in 1998, a recording of a homecoming gig at Glasgow's King's Theatre. Connolly reflected on his local upbringing and took his audience with him, metaphorically, on a nostalgia trip around local locations. The routine had some inevitable tweaking of subject matter as would be expected, but despite the routines about old age, there were still the familiar wickedly funny observations on drunks and the British class barriers. There was a further bonus for Connolly fans in 2000 when TV audiences saw a guest appearance on the US sci-fi sitcom *Third Rock from the Sun.*

Billy Connolly's *World Tour of England, Ireland and Wales* began with him sailing up the Liffey, reflecting on the beauty of Guinness despite his years off the sauce. But this was no twee tourist version of Irish experience, a point Connolly was keen to emphasise when visiting Blarney Castle and refusing to kiss the famous stone that is supposed to give the kisser the gift of the gab. But then, why on earth would he? Instead, Connolly settled for explaining how the stone had been a gift from Robert the Bruce for help received in defeating the English at Bannockburn, after which Billy speculated whether there had been a mix-up in the present list, with the lump of granite being sent in place of a precious gem. There was a visit to Kilmainham prison on the outskirts of Dublin, where 14 leaders of the Easter Rising of 1916 were executed, a poignant meeting with the mother of former Thin Lizzy singer Phil Lynott by his graveside, and a tour of the ailing Belfast shipyards, which clearly struck a chord with Connolly's own personal history.

In Wales, Connolly purred over the resurrection of Cardiff with its posh new stadium, revitalised dock area and striking modern public

ON YER BIKE

art, showing that he was far from a Luddite who was interested in nostalgia for nostalgia's sake.

On the English leg, Connolly was enthralled by the works of art painted by north-eastern miners in the early twentieth century, now on display at the mining museum at Ashington. He startled passengers on the London Underground by appearing from the door that leads to the drivers' cab (he'd earlier greeted the driver with a modest but presumably unnecessary "Hi, I'm Billy Connolly"), only to realise that he's now stuffed because he hasn't got a ticket. And he climbed the tower of Big Ben in a sequence that, if nothing else, led to a great one liner in the live footage: "I went up Big Ben today. Sounds like I'm coming out doesn't it?"

Fans of Connolly's *World Tours* have more to look forward to in 2004 with the screening of the latest in the series – Billy Connolly's *World Tour of New Zealand*. Among the escapades the Big Yin got up to – at the tender age of 61 when filming took place – was being thrown from a 600ft high building while attached to a wire harness. Connolly played 14 venues plus a number of secret pub gigs in February and March of 2003 to record footage for the shows, which programme-makers were hoping would stretch to between 10 and 13 episodes. *Billy Connolly's World Tours* are a fun and warm journey through the things that light Billy's fire and the New Zealand shows will be a welcome return to British TV screens.

The *World Tours* weren't Billy's only location filming for TV during the Nineties. There would also be some much more serious programmes to be made (as well as some that turned out to be plain daft), and all in the name of charity. And they'd all involve putting on a big red nose.

10

Charity work

BILLY CONNOLLY

CHARITY WORK

T here are a number of ways that artistes can have their contribution to popular culture honoured. Sometimes it's a Lifetime Achievement BAFTA, at other times it's an appearance on *This Is Your Life*. But for a music lover probably nothing better than being asked on the utterly indulgent *Desert Island Discs*. Billy Connolly was invited to be a castaway on the Radio 4 institution in July 2002. The programme is unusual in its range of guests: one week it can be a ridiculously famous pop star, the next a not especially liked politician, the next an obscure poet known only to readers of *The Sunday Times*. But

CHARITY WORK

one prerequisite is that the guest should have had an interesting life and/or plenty to say for themselves, because the musical element is interspersed with chat with host Sue Lawley. Billy Connolly, of course, has both.

The set-up of the show is simple: guests are asked to imagine themselves cast-away on a fictitious desert island and to choose eight records they would take with them, plus a book (apart from the *Bible* and the *Complete Works of Shakespeare*, both supplied automatically and indicate the show's middle class sensibilities) and a luxury. The show has traditionally been heavily weighted towards classical music, guided by the choices of its guests, often punctuated by a token rock song or two. The list of another son of Glasgow, former foreign secretary Robin Cook, was typical, including Mahler, Khactaturian and Wagner alongside Bob Dylan. In recent years, following Tony Blair's declaration that we all live in Cool Britannia, the tradition has been somewhat reversed, with relatively safe lists of rock sons punctuated with classical references for an air of intellectualism. When Billy Connolly went on the show there were no such considerations: it was an honest list of the songs

CHARITY WORK

that turned him on. With memories of his childhood and his own earliest performing influences there was the other-worldly voice of country star Hank Williams singing *Long Gone Lonesome Blues*, the record singled out by Connolly as the one he'd most like to have if allowed only one. Roy Orbison offered another distinctive vocal style with *Only the Lonely*. The early passion for rock 'n' roll was acknowledged with Little Richard's *Tutti Frutti*. There was nothing particularly original in picking a Beatles track, but *Across the Universe* was a lightly offbeat choice. Then there was *Highlands* by Bob Dylan, *Foggy Mountain Breakdown* by the legendary bluegrass combo Flatt and Scruggs, and *Morris Room* by folk group The Celebrated Ratliffe Stout Band. No Brahms or Liszt: the closest he got to a classical reference was with the Regimental Band & Massed Pipes of the Scots Guards playing the *Skye Boat Song*. Connolly's love of music was even evident in his choice of one luxury to take on the island: he plumped for his banjo, enabling him to provide his own soundtrack if he wished. For the record, his choice of book was the *Oxford English Dictionary*.

The Big Yin's ability and willingness to talk

CHARITY WORK

made him a natural choice for any broadcaster looking for guests for their shows. And his popularity with the general public has made him a useful tool when the aim of the broadcast is to get people to part with their money. Billy is always happy to support good causes and has been involved in several Comic Relief Red Nose Days over the years. The most notorious was in 2001 when the 58-year-old comic streaked naked around Piccadilly Circus in the heart of London. Some more sensitive souls failed to see the funny side and the Broadcasting Standards Commission received complaints from 70 of the 12.6 million viewers who tuned in to see the festivities. Luckily the BSC didn't forget the spirit of the occasion and rejected the viewers' complaints about the stunt, which contributed to the year's £61-million fundraising effort. The authorities recognised it for what it was: "a harmless piece of fun". If the streaking episode represented Connolly at his most outrageous, other Comic Relief appeals have revealed his more serious and thoughtful side. In 1995, he filed an on-the-spot report from war-torn Mozambique with a follow-up the following year. For 2003 he returned to Africa, for a programme focusing on a week in the life of a hospital in

CHARITY WORK

Somalia, the world's third poorest country.

Of course, plenty of comedians (as well as assorted newsreaders, weathermen and soap stars) have jumped on the charity bandwagon, but Connolly's films for Comic Relief showed that he was clearly moved by what he saw. It wasn't enough for him to be contributing to the bigger show business event. Connolly decided that more could be done and that he was the one to do it. As tea was now the favourite drink of the Big Yin, Connolly decided it would be an appropriate commercial activity to raise money for those less fortunate than himself. The tea shares its name with his management company, Tickety Boo, and quickly found its way on to the shelves of some of the UK's biggest supermarket chains. A portion of the sale of every packet has already helped house 50 neglected and abandoned children in India, and has also helped children in China, Romania and Tibet. The day after launching the tea on board the *Grand Turk*, a square-rigged ship used in the BBC TV series *Hornblower*, Connolly began a 25-date-sell-out run at the Hammersmith Apollo, demonstrating that there was still as big a thirst for his live shows as for his beverages. A couple of months earlier he'd played the best part of 60 gigs

CHARITY WORK

across Australia and New Zealand. A new song appeared in the shows, the *Tickety-Boo Tea Song*, a healthy plug for the charitable cause. The song was co-written with good friend Ralph McTell, the man who had brought the world *The Streets of London* in 1974. For a long time Billy had told a tale of how the singer had once got lost trying to give Billy directions as they were driving round the capital!

As well as supporting good causes abroad, Billy has never forgotten his working class Glasgow roots, despite accusations from sections of the Scottish press. When Glasgow's nineteenth century sewerage system collapsed following sustained torrential rain in 2002, much of the East End of the city flooded. Many people were left with nothing, as their possessions were washed away and they were uninsured. The Big Yin was touched by their plight and stepped in to play *Welly Aid*, a series of three dates at Glasgow's cavernous SECC, to raise money for the victims. Although previously Connolly had been scathing about the overall role of the Scottish Parliament, its members weren't prepared to let that bit of history stand in the way of recognising *Welly Aid*'s contribution to easing the crisis. A motion as tabled which read: "The Parliament

CHARITY WORK

joins with the people of Glasgow's East End in expressing profound thanks to Mr Billy Connolly for his magnificent effort in raising funds for the East End flood victims; is mindful of the time he gave up for free to play the SECC on three successive nights to packed audiences and how his gesture raised not only funds but also the hearts of people in Glasgow left with no possessions after devastating flooding, and salutes this international star as a true son of Glasgow, who returned to his roots at the moment intervention was most needed." Not the most eloquent of citations, granted, but it's the thought that counts.

In 1998, Billy and Pamela bought the Candacraig Estate in the Highlands, making Billy a laird. He took his role seriously and made many friends among the locals three years later when he donated the proceeds from a concert in Aberdeen towards the repair of the village hall roof.

Billy was touched by another moving story from his homeland in 2003. A young Scottish woman named Millie Forbes was suffering from a deadly form of leukaemia and had launched her own campaign to raise awareness of the disease and increase the numbers of people coming forward to offer themselves as potential bone

CHARITY WORK

marrow donors. Millie had already received chemotherapy treatment, but the leukaemia had returned and a bone marrow transplant was the only future course available to her. The search for a donor had already moved to the US as the trail had run dry in the UK. Billy did a photoshoot and cracked jokes with reporters, raising spirits in the campaign and awareness of Millie's plight. A donor was found for Millie through the Anthony Nolan Trust and she received a stem cell transplant in December 2003. The campaign continues.

Despite much press hostility north of the border, Billy's affection for Scotland was largely reciprocated. Wherever he has played in the world, ex-pat Scots have formed a large chunk of his constituency. When he played the groundbreaking London Palladium gig back in 1975 the audience was largely a sell-out because tickets were snapped up by exiled Scots. Billy's roots and his contribution to Scottish cultural and civic life were formally recognised in 2001, when the Big Yin was given an honourary degree by Glasgow University. The institution was marking its 550th anniversary by honouring a number of men who had all started out in the Clydeside shipyards in the Fifties and Sixties. Forty-plus years on from when Billy had

CHARITY WORK

first stepped foot in them, the yards were not the bustling industrial centres they once were, and as Billy went up to receive his award, it was against a backdrop of further redundancies. Connolly made the most of the opportunity to speak of his sadness over the yards' fate. "They [the government] should have got behind the Clyde," he said. "It takes my breath away how little they value it." Addressing the audience at the ceremony, the university's dean of arts astutely observed that "contrary to those who mutter 'sell-out', one of the things we might most admire about Billy Connolly is his ability to reinvent himself without losing what it was he started with."

This quality is there for all to see in Connolly's most recent TV project, an on-going sequence of programmes that puts Billy on his beloved Harley motorbike and takes viewers on a journey around the world.

11

The future

BILLY CONNOLLY

THE FUTURE

One of the most talked-about events in rural Scottish life in recent years was when pop superstar Madonna married film director Guy Ritchie at Skibo Castle in December 2000. The castle was besieged by the media, chasing a glimpse of the happy couple and their glamourous guests. But whatever showbiz pull the couple managed to display in their guest list, there was someone planning a party with one or two people that would blow Mr and Mrs Ritchie away.

Billy Connolly, the wild man of British comedy for three decades, hit his 60th birthday in November 2002. Perhaps with an eye on the

THE FUTURE

unattractiveness of the Highlands to pampered stars at the onset of winter, Billy and Pamela chose to celebrate the occasion in August with a party at their rural retreat, the 15-bedroom Candacraig House in Aberdeenshire. The couple had bought the country estate in 1998 from Body Shop founder Anita Roddick, soon after Billy had fallen in love with the area while filming *Mrs Brown*. In the summer of 2003, it was reported by the Scottish press that Connolly, a fan of Scotland's stone circles, had had a three-ton granite standing stone erected in the grounds with the words: "There is no such thing as normal" etched on it. In the *World Tour of Scotland* programmes he'd danced naked round a stone circle in Orkney. The stone carver, Martin Cook, was invited to stay with Billy and Pamela during the work. "It was fantastic," Cook told the *Daily Record*. "Billy and his wife are delightful people. Incredibly hospitable and what you see with him on TV is absolutely how he is."

Back at the party, the guest list included Michael Parkinson and Dame Judi Dench, plus Hollywood pals Robin Williams and Steve Martin. The broadcaster and Labour minister Lord (Gus) McDonald, who'd received an honourary degree

THE FUTURE

from Glasgow University at the same time as Connolly, was there too. Bob Geldof and former world motor racing champion Jackie Stewart were also among the 200 guests. And then there was Prince Charles, accompanied by Camilla Parker-Bowles. It wasn't exactly a surprise that Charles should accept the invitation, because Billy and Pamela had long been known to have royal connections, in particular a well-documented friendship with Prince Andrew and Sarah Ferguson before and after they became the Duke and Duchess of York. Billy and Pamela had been guests at Andrew and Sarah's wedding.

Of course, anyone can invite the heir to the throne to a party, but getting him to turn up is another matter. It only served to emphasise how far from the Clyde shipyards the one-time apprentice welder had come. It was also a demonstration of the ease with which Connolly has been able to cross class boundaries throughout his life, unfazed by the status or glamour of those around him; he's equally at home in the Scotia Bar in Glasgow where he used to hang out in his folk days or the grounds of Buck House. "I just accept friendship where it's offered. I don't care who people are," he said in 1999.

BILLY CONNOLLY

THE FUTURE

Like most people with that degree of fame, there's sometimes a price to pay. During his career, Connolly has had to endure flack from the Scottish press, the prying of members of the public during his time living in Bray and media gossip over his relationships with Pamela or his mother. The latest unwelcome attention has come from quite another quarter, with Connolly's name and Candacraig House alongside other celebrity entries on a hitlist for anti-bloodsports' campaigners. Connolly is a keen angler and Candacraig Estate includes a trout lake, although Billy is on record as saying there's nothing like the feeling of releasing a trout back into the water. Generally, Connolly has taken to his duties as laird with his usual vigour, including opening a children's playground at Timontoul and attending the local Highland Games. Although there were some mutterings that Billy's famous guests were distracting spectators from the athletic activities, Connolly proved a popular figure with the games' organiser, being made an honourary member of the Lonach Highland Society in recognition of his services to the area, a privilege which allows him to process with the participants as they make their way to the games.

BILLY CONNOLLY

THE FUTURE

Most people are prepared to settle for what they've achieved by the time they reach 60, but for Billy Connolly the milestone seems to have kick-started another phase in his career. Working with Tom Cruise on *The Last Samurai* has raised his stock in Hollywood. He's in line to play Uncle Monty, in a film of the children's story *A Series of Unfortunate Events* by Lemony Snicket, a part which is being reported to put him in the $1-million-a-movie bracket, up there with chums Sean Connery and Michael Caine. As the books number 10 volumes in all, a box office smash for the film would surely see it pencilled in for sequels in Harry Potter style. And maybe we'll see Billy himself in future Harry Potter flicks. His fans would certainly like to think so, with an online petition started to persuade the film's producers to give Connolly the part of wizard hunter Mad Eye Moody in the forthcoming *Harry Potter And The Goblet of Fire.*

Connolly was filming again in 2003, this time with a part in a spoof of the Merchant Ivory period dramas, directed by former Monty Python star Eric Idle, a friend of Billy's. When the public will get to see *The Remains of the Piano*, if at all, is a mystery. The movie enjoys a star-studded cast but

THE FUTURE

is resting in the Warner Brothers vaults with no release date planned. The doubt over its future left Idle lamenting the death of George Harrison, whose HandMade films had brought other ex-Python projects to the screen. In *The Remains of the Piano*, Connolly plays Police Inspector MacGuffin, alongside *Star Trek* skipper Patrick Stewart, Anjelica Huston and Orlando Bloom. The main part of Hopkins, a man who brings a piano back from colonial India, is taken by Geoffrey Rush of *Shine* fame. Tim Curry, who Connolly supported in *Muppet Treasure Island*, is also in it as Reverend Whoopsie. Billy's close friend and admirer Robin Williams also has a cameo role.

The films will no doubt keep on coming – the great thing about the movies is that they'll always be arts for anyone of whatever age. But the public will never be happier than when Billy Connolly is making their sides ache with laughter. Connolly's stand-up may have become more restrained with age, but it contains the same energy and empathy that it always did and still draws on the same fertile comedy ground that Billy sees around him every day, still raging against the beige people in the world. Pamela has noted that Billy never seems happier than when he's on stage doing

THE FUTURE

stand-up and many of his fans would share his feelings. Even in his seventh decade and with acting work galore, there's no sign that the stand-up will become a thing of the past, although a tour of New Zealand in early 2004 was limited to a mere 25 dates compared to the 80- or 90-odd dates that he might have done in years gone by. Connolly also did two dates at the Oxford New Theatre in Britain in memory of the late Malcom Kingsnorth, who was his tour manager and sound engineer for 25 years.

The big banana boots will not be putting in an appearance, however, as they're already consigned to a place in history, as an exhibit in a Glasgow museum. But there is one slightly strange Glaswegian who's prepared to carry on the banana boot tradition. Gary Moir is one of a band of individuals promoting themselves as Billy Connolly tribute acts, an honour more usually reserved for notable pop and rock groups like the Beatles, the Doors or Abba. Curiously, Moir is a "failed welder" who performed as a singer and comedian in small venues around Glasgow (and whose songs included *Stick Yer Weldin' Rods Up Yir Arse*), before it ever occurred to him to do it in the guise of Connolly. You have to be popular to

THE FUTURE

have a tribute act, and you've got to be particularly well-liked to have three. Rick Toner fills the demand for bum gags and silly songs in New Zealand when the real Billy isn't in town and calls himself Willy Connory. But perhaps the most high-profile lookalike is Cambridgeshire council worker Bob Lucas, alias Barely Connery, whose exploits have taken him on to ITV's *Stars And Their Doubles Programme*. "The good thing is he's so popular, you are going to get a good response", Lucas told the *Cambridge News* in 2002, referring to the real Billy. Connolly has also inspired some other unlikely performers, including Scottish junior football player Neil Ward of Forth Wanderers, who told the *Daily Record* in 2004: "I have always tried to play the clown and the lads are a willing audience. Most guys of my generation had Kenny Dalglish and Charlie Nicholas as their idols but mine were Billy Connolly and Spike Milligan."

Billy has been happy to pay public tribute to others he admires. In 2003, he appeared in a BBC TV special about the life and work of musician Richard Thompson. "He's a quiet guy," observed Connolly. "He's almost an anorak, our Richard. You wouldn't think he's the guy with the guitar shaking the town." You'd certainly never be left in much doubt if Connolly was the guy shaking the town. His own presence and popularity has also made the real Billy a natural choice for advertisers wanting a personality to publicise their products. The best ad – arguably one of the cheekiest poster campaigns of all times – remains the Wonderbra spoof for Kaliber, but in more recent times he's appeared as a mysterious lake-dwelling wizard-god as the public face of a credit card called Goldfish. Then he was asked to become the public voice of the National Lottery on its relaunch in 2002, urging punters "Don't live a little, live a lotto." Of course, no one can have universal acclaim with everything they become involved with, and Connolly was unfortunate to get on board the National Lottery bandwagon as the wheels were starting to fall off. The campaign was pulled and named the most annoying ad of the year by the industry magazine *Marketing*. But the ads clearly did their job, with 83 per cent of people able to recall seeing it in the previous week according to advertising industry surveys.

As the birthday bash showed, the Big Yin has collected a host of show business pals over the years, one of whom is Michael Parkinson. Billy still drops in on the *Parkinson* show, where it all really

THE FUTURE

began for Billy the comic. Indeed, he was one of the first names on the guest list when the show was revived by the Beeb in the late Nineties. After a break during the Nineties, the chat show host was brought back from his exile in print and on radio at the start of a new century, and the Big Yin was still a sure-fire way to put noughts on the ratings. Pamela appeared with him on his last outing in which he revealed that he'd had a tattoo of a row of pansies across both his feet, inspired he claimed, by a Glaswegian who had only half an arm with the words "to be continued" tattooed on it.

It's for astute observations of real life such as this that Connolly manages to top those polls of comic heroes. A public survey by the whisky company Famous Grouse at Christmas 2003, named Connolly along with pop singer Robbie Williams, as top of the wanted list to have as a guest at a Christmas party, ahead of Jonny Wilkinson who'd just won the rugby World Cup for England. David Beckham and Nelson Mandela were both left trailing in Billy and Robbie's wakes. A poll in the *Sunday Herald* in Scotland in January 2004 saw Connolly voted as the third greatest living Scot, behind only Sean Connery and the Scottish socialist leader Tommy Sheridan.

BILLY CONNOLLY

THE FUTURE

Manchester United manager Sir Alex Ferguson was way down in eighth place. The newspaper speculated that Connolly could have won had he not belittled the country's "wee pretendy Parliament", although one of the published voter citations suggested he was "a great ambassador for the country". Connolly's dismissal of the Scottish Parliament had begun five years earlier when he turned down an invitation to its opening. One Scottish institution that he does have more time for is Celtic Football Club and one of his prouder moments came in 1996 when he was invited to open a new stand there and was given a seat for life.

If Billy does decide to slow down it might be so that he can spend more time with his grandchildren. There's only one so far – Cara's son Walter who was born in 2001, but with five children of his own, one suspects there may eventually be more. Walter and subsequent siblings or cousins may well have the unusual privilege of settling down to watch a Disney film on DVD and hearing their granddad's voice coming out of the character's mouths. Billy played Ben the Sailor in his own Glaswegian brogue in the movie *Pocahontas*.

BILLY CONNOLLY

THE FUTURE

Whatever happens the pipe and carpet slippers will remain firmly under wraps. "I still feel 35," he said in an interview soon after his 60th birthday. "I still feel sexy. I don't mean I feel I'm a sexy man like Sean Connery, but I still feel sexual." He also said: "I find myself gasping every time I get up or sit down. But overall I feel good. My attitude to ageing is completely unprepared and I would like it to remain that way." The move into middle age hasn't made his observations any less current: Simon Cowell and the Pop Idol phenomenon were a recent target.

A man like Connolly, who waits until he's in his 50s to have his nipples pierced and dye his beard purple, is hardly on the verge of joining the Darby and Joan Club. The 2004 tour was wryly named the *Too Old To Die Young* tour, indicating an awareness of the passing of time without the willingness to surrender to it. Two decades ago, the Big Yin signed off *An Audience with Billy Connolly* by saying his guests had "made a happy man very old". If he does ever retire he might look back at his career and feel that the more traditional order of that saying is more appropriate. But don't expect that to happen just yet. Billy Connolly will be determined not to grow beige before his time.

12

Discography

BILLY CONNOLLY

DISCOGRAPHY

Singles

Shoeshine Boy (with The Humblebums 1970)

D.I.V.O.R.C.E. (highest chart position 1,
Nov 1975)

No Chance (No charge) (24, July 1976)

In the Brownies (38, Aug 1979)

Super Gran (32, March 1985)

Freedom (with Chris Tummings, did not chart)
1985

Irish Heartbeat (did not chart) 1990

Albums

First Collection of Merry Melodies
(with The Humblebums 1969)

The New Humblebums
(with The Humblebums 1969)

Open Up the Door
(with The Humblebums 1970)

Solo Concert (1974)

Cop Yer Whack For This (1974)

Live (1995)

13

TV appearances

BILLY CONNOLLY

TV APPEARANCES

TV drama
Just Another Sunday (1975)
The Elephant's Graveyard (1977)
Androcles and the Lion (1983)
Down Among the Big Boys (1993)
The Life and Times of Deacon Brodie (1996)
The Life and Times of Deacon Brodie (1996)
Gentleman's Relish (2001)

TV documentary
This Is Your Life (1980)
South Bank Show (1992)
The Bigger Picture (1994)
A Scot in the Arctic (1995)
Billy Connolly's World Tour of Scotland (1995)
Billy Connolly's World Tour of Australia (1996)

TV comedy
Billy Connolly in Concert (1978)
A Weekend in Wallop (1984)
An Audience With Billy Connolly (1985)
Head of the Class (1990–91)
Billy (1992)
Billy Connolly, Erect For 30 Years (1998)
One Night Stand (1998)
World Tour of England, Ireland and Wales (2002)

14

Live shows and theatre

BILLY CONNOLLY

LIVE SHOWS AND THEATRE

Major live shows

London Palladium (1975)

Elton John Tour, USA (1976)

The Secret Policeman's Ball (1981)

The Secret Policeman's Other Ball (1982)

Royal Albert Hall (1988)

Nelson Mandela 70th birthday concert (1988)

Record-breaking run at Hammersmith Odeon, London (1994)

Theatre

The Great Northern Welly Boot Show (1974)

And Me Wi' Me Bad Leg Tae (1976)

Groan Up (1977)

When Hair was Long (1977)

The Beastly Beatitudes of Balthazar B

15

Filmography

BILLY CONNOLLY

FILMOGRAPHY

Big Banana Feet (concert footage) (1976)
Absolution (1981)
Bullshot (1983)
Water (1985)
The Big Man (1990)
Indecent Proposal (1993)
Pocahontas (1995)
Muppet Treasure Island (1996)
Middleton's Changeling (1997)
Mrs Brown (1997)
Paws (1997)
The Imposters (1998)
Still Crazy (1998)
The Boondock Saints (1999)
The Debt Collector (1999)
Beautiful Joe (2000)
An Everlasting Piece (2000)
Gabriel & and Me (2001)
The Man Who Sued God (2001)
Timeline (2003)
The Last Samurai (2003)

BIOGRAPHIES

OTHER BOOKS IN THE SERIES

Also available in the series:

OTHER BOOKS IN THE SERIES

JENNIFER ANISTON

She's been a Friend to countless millions worldwide, and overcame numerous hurdles to rise to the very top of her field. From a shy girl with a dream of being a famous actress, through being reduced to painting scenery for high school plays, appearing in a series of flop TV shows and one rather bad movie, Jennifer Aniston has persevered, finally finding success at the very top of the TV tree.

Bringing the same determination that got her a part on the world's best-loved TV series to her attempts at a film career, she's also worked her way from rom-com cutie up to serious, respected actress and box office draw, intelligently combining indie, cult and comedy movies into a blossoming career which looks set to shoot her to the heights of Hollywood's A-list. She's also found love with one of the world's most desirable men. Is Jennifer Aniston the ultimate Hollywood Renaissance woman? It would seem she's got more than a shot at such a title, as indeed, she seems to have it all, even if things weren't always that way. Learn all about Aniston's rise to fame in this compelling biography.

OTHER BOOKS IN THE SERIES

DAVID BECKHAM

This book covers the amazing life of the boy from East London who has not only become a world class footballer and the captain of England, but also an idol to millions, and probably the most famous man in Britain.

His biography tracks his journey, from the playing fields of Chingford to the Bernabau. It examines how he joined his beloved Manchester United and became part of a golden generation of talent that led to United winning trophies galore.

Beckham's parallel personal life is also examined, as he moved from tongue-tied football-obsessed kid to suitor of a Spice Girl, to one half of Posh & Becks, the most famous celebrity couple in Britain – perhaps the world. His non-footballing activities, his personal indulgences and changing styles have invited criticism, and even abuse, but his football talent has confounded the critics, again and again.

The biography looks at his rise to fame and his relationship with Posh, as well as his decision to leave Manchester for Madrid. Has it affected his relationship with Posh? What will the latest controversy over his sex life mean for celebrity's royal couple? And will he come back to play in England again?

OTHER BOOKS IN THE SERIES

GEORGE CLOONEY

The tale of George Clooney's astonishing career is an epic every bit as riveting as one of his blockbuster movies. It's a story of tenacity and determination, of fame and infamy, a story of succeeding on your own terms regardless of the risks. It's also a story of emergency rooms, batsuits, tidal waves and killer tomatoes, but let's not get ahead of ourselves.

Born into a family that, by Sixties' Kentucky standards, was dripping with show business glamour, George grew up seeing the hard work and heartache that accompanied a life in the media spotlight.

By the time stardom came knocking for George Clooney, it found a level-headed and mature actor ready and willing to embrace the limelight, while still indulging a lifelong love of partying and practical jokes. A staunchly loyal friend and son, a bachelor with a taste for the high life, a vocal activist for the things he believes and a born and bred gentleman; through failed sitcoms and blockbuster disasters, through artistic credibility and box office success, George Clooney has remained all of these things...and much, much more. Prepare to meet Hollywood's most fascinating megastar in this riveting biography.

OTHER BOOKS IN THE SERIES

ROBERT DE NIRO

Robert De Niro is cinema's greatest chameleon. Snarling one minute, smirking the next, he's straddled Hollywood for a quarter of a century, making his name as a serious character actor, in roles ranging from psychotic taxi drivers to hardened mobsters. The scowls and pent-up violence may have won De Niro early acclaim but, ingeniously, he's now playing them for laughs, poking fun at the tough guy image he so carefully cultivated. Ever the perfectionist, De Niro holds nothing back on screen, but in real life he is a very private man – he thinks of himself as just another guy doing a job. Some job, some guy. There's more to the man than just movies. De Niro helped New York pick itself up after the September 11 terrorist attacks on the Twin Towers by launching the TriBeCa Film Festival and inviting everyone downtown. He runs several top-class restaurants and has dated some of the most beautiful women in the world, least of all supermodel Naomi Campbell. Now in his 60s, showered with awards and a living legend, De Niro's still got his foot on the pedal. There are six, yes six, films coming your way in 2004. In this latest biography, you'll discover all about his latest roles and the life of this extraordinary man.

OTHER BOOKS IN THE SERIES

MICHAEL DOUGLAS

Douglas may have been a shaggy-haired member of a hippy commune in the Sixties but just like all the best laidback, free-loving beatniks, he's gone on to blaze a formidable career, in both acting and producing.

In a career that has spanned nearly 40 years so far, Douglas has produced a multitude of hit movies including the classic *One Flew Over The Cuckoo's Nest* and *The China Syndrome* through to box office smashes such as *Starman* and *Face/Off*.

His acting career has been equally successful – from *Romancing The Stone* to *Wall Street* to *Fatal Attraction*, Douglas's roles have shown that he isn't afraid of putting himself on the line when up there on the big screen.

His relationship with his father; his stay in a top clinic to combat his drinking problem; the breakdown of his first marriage; and his publicised clash with the British media have all compounded to create the image of a man who's transformed himself from being the son of Hollywood legend Kirk Douglas, into Kirk Douglas being the dad of Hollywood legend, Michael Douglas.

OTHER BOOKS IN THE SERIES

HUGH GRANT

He's the Oxford fellow who stumbled into acting, the middle-class son of a carpet salesman who became famous for bumbling around stately homes and posh weddings. The megastar actor who claims he doesn't like acting, but has appeared in over 40 movies and TV shows.

On screen he's romanced a glittering array of Hollywood's hottest actresses, and tackled medical conspiracies and the mafia. Off screen he's hogged the headlines with his high profile girlfriend as well as finding lifelong notoriety after a little Divine intervention in Los Angeles.

Hugh Grant is Britain's biggest movie star, an actor whose talent for comedy has often been misjudged by those who assume he simply plays himself.

From bit parts in Nottingham theatre, through comedy revues at the Edinburgh Fringe, and on to the top of the box office charts, Hugh has remained constant – charming, witty and ever so slightly sarcastic, obsessed with perfection and performance while winking to his audience as if to say: "This is all awfully silly, isn't it?" Don't miss this riveting biography.

OTHER BOOKS IN THE SERIES

MICHAEL JACKSON

Friday 29 August 1958 was not a special day in Gary, Indiana, and indeed Gary, was far from being a special place. But it was on this day and in this location that the world's greatest entertainer was to be born, Michael Joseph Jackson.

The impact that this boy was destined to have on the world of entertainment could never have been estimated. Here we celebrate Michael Jackson's extraordinary talents, and plot the defining events over his 40-year career. This biography explores the man behind the myth, and gives an understanding of what drives this special entertainer.

In 1993, there was an event that was to rock Jackson's world. His friendship with a 12-year-old boy and the subsequent allegations resulted in a lawsuit, a fall in record sales and a long road to recovery. Two marriages, three children and 10 years later there is a feeling of déjà vu as Jackson again deals with more controversy. Without doubt, 2004 proves to be the most important year in the singer's life. Whatever that future holds for Jackson, his past is secured, there has never been and there will never again be anything quite like Michael Jackson.

OTHER BOOKS IN THE SERIES

NICOLE KIDMAN

On 23 March 2003 Nicole Kidman won the Oscar for Best Actress for her role as Virginia Woolf in *The Hours*. That was the night that marked Nicole Kidman's acceptance into the upper echelons of Hollywood royalty. She had certainly come a long way from the 'girlfriend' roles she played when she first arrived in Hollywood – in films such as *Billy Bathgate* and *Batman Forever* – although even then she managed to inject her 'pretty girl' roles with an edge that made her acting stand out. And she was never merely content to be Mrs Cruise, movie star's wife. Although she stood dutifully behind her then husband in 1993 when he was given his star on the Hollywood Walk of Fame, Nicole got a star of her own 10 years later, in 2003.

Not only does Nicole Kidman have stunning good looks and great pulling power at the box office, she also has artistic credibility. But Nicole has earned the respect of her colleagues, working hard and turning in moving performances from a very early age. Although she dropped out of school at 16, no one doubts the intelligence and passion that are behind the fiery redhead's acting career, which includes television and stage work, as well as films. Find out how Kidman became one of Hollywood's most respected actresses in this compelling biography.

OTHER BOOKS IN THE SERIES

JENNIFER LOPEZ

There was no suggestion that the Jennifer Lopez of the early Nineties would become the accomplished actress, singer and icon that she is today. Back then she was a dancer on the popular comedy show *In Living Color* – one of the Fly Girls, the accompaniment, not the main event. In the early days she truly was Jenny from the block; the Bronx native of Puerto Rican descent – another hopeful from the east coast pursuing her dreams in the west.

Today, with two marriages under her belt, three multi-platinum selling albums behind her and an Oscar-winning hunk as one of her ex-boyfriends, she is one of the most talked about celebrities of the day. Jennifer Lopez is one of the most celebrated Hispanic actresses of all time.

Her beauty, body and famous behind, are lusted after by men and envied by women throughout the world. She has proven that she can sing, dance and act. Yet her critics dismiss her as a diva without talent. And the criticisms are not just about her work, some of them are personal. But what is the reality? Who is Jennifer Lopez, where did she come from and how did get to where she is now? This biography aims to separate fact from fiction to reveal the real Jennifer Lopez.

OTHER BOOKS IN THE SERIES

MADONNA

Everyone thought they had Madonna figured out in early 2003. The former Material Girl had become Maternal Girl, giving up on causing controversy to look after her two children and set up home in England with husband Guy Ritchie. The former wild child had settled down and become respectable. The new Madonna would not do anything to shock the establishment anymore, she'd never do something like snogging both Britney Spears and Christina Aguilera at the MTV Video Music Awards... or would she?

Of course she would. Madonna has been constantly reinventing herself since she was a child, and her ability to shock even those who think they know better is both a tribute to her business skills and the reason behind her staying power. Only Madonna could create gossip with two of the current crop of pop princesses in August and then launch a children's book in September. In fact, only Madonna would even try.

In her 20-year career she has not just been a successful pop singer, she is also a movie star, a business woman, a stage actress, an author and a mother. Find out all about this extraordinary modern-day icon in this new compelling biography.

OTHER BOOKS IN THE SERIES

BRAD PITT

From the launch pad that was his scene stealing turn in *Thelma And Louise* as the sexual-enlightening bad boy. To his character-driven performances in dramas such as *Legends of the Fall* through to his Oscar-nominated work in *Twelve Monkeys* and the dark and razor-edged Tyler Durden in *Fight Club*, Pitt has never rested on his laurels. Or his good looks.

And the fact that his love life has garnered headlines all over the world hasn't hindered Brad Pitt's profile away from the screen either – linked by the press to many women, his relationships with the likes of Juliette Lewis and Gwyneth Paltrow. Then of course, in 2000, we had the Hollywood fairytale ending when he tied the silk knot with Jennifer Aniston.

Pitt's impressive track record as a superstar, sex symbol *and* credible actor looks set to continue as he has three films lined up for release over the next year – as Achilles in the Wolfgang Peterson-helmed Troy; Rusty Ryan in the sequel *Ocean's Twelve* and the titular Mr Smith in the thriller *Mr & Mrs Smith* alongside Angelina Jolie. Pitt's ever-growing success shows no signs of abating. Discover all about Pitt's meteoric rise from rags to riches in this riveting biography.

OTHER BOOKS IN THE SERIES

SHANE RICHIE

Few would begrudge the current success of 40-year-old Shane Richie. To get where he is today, Shane has had a rather bumpy roller coaster ride that has seen the hard working son of poor Irish immigrants endure more than his fair share of highs and lows – financially, professionally and personally.

In the space of four decades he has amused audiences at school plays, realised his childhood dream of becoming a Pontins holiday camp entertainer, experienced homelessness, beat his battle with drink, became a million-aire then lost the lot. He's worked hard and played hard.

When the producers of *EastEnders* auditioned Shane for a role in the top TV soap, they decided not to give him the part, but to create a new character especially for him. That character was Alfie Moon, manager of the Queen Vic pub, and very quickly Shane's TV alter ego has become one of the most popular soap characters in Britain. This biography is the story of a boy who had big dreams and never gave up on turning those dreams into reality

OTHER BOOKS IN THE SERIES

JONNY WILKINSON

"There's 35 seconds to go, this is the one. It's coming back for Jonny Wilkinson. He drops for World Cup glory. It's over! He's done it! Jonny Wilkinson is England's Hero yet again..."

That memorable winning drop kick united the nation, and lead to the start of unprecedented victory celebrations throughout the land. In the split seconds it took for the ball to leave his boot and slip through the posts, Wilkinson's life was to change forever. It wasn't until three days later, when the squad flew back to Heathrow and were met with a rapturous reception, that the enormity of their win, began to sink in.

Like most overnight success stories, Wilkinson's journey has been a long and dedicated one. He spent 16 years 'in rehearsal' before achieving his finest performance, in front of a global audience of 22 million, on that rainy evening in Telstra Stadium, Sydney.

But how did this modest self-effacing 24-year-old become England's new number one son? This biography follows Jonny's journey to international stardom. Find out how he caught the rugby bug, what and who his earliest influences were and what the future holds for our latest English sporting hero.

OTHER BOOKS IN THE SERIES

ROBBIE WILLIAMS

Professionally, things can't get much better for Robbie Williams. In 2002 he signed the largest record deal in UK history when he re-signed with EMI. The following year he performed to over 1.5 million fans on his European tour, breaking all attendance records at Knebworth with three consecutive sell-out gigs.

Since going solo Robbie Williams has achieved five number one hit singles, five number one hit albums; 10 Brits and three Ivor Novello awards. When he left the highly successful boy band Take That in 1995 his future seemed far from rosy. He got off to a shaky start. His nemesis, Gary Barlow, had already recorded two number one singles and the press had virtually written Williams off. But then in December 1997, he released his Christmas single, *Angels*.

Angels re-launched his career – it remained in the Top 10 for 11 weeks. Since then Robbie has gone from strength to strength, both as a singer and a natural showman. His live videos are a testament to his performing talent and his promotional videos are works of art.

This biography tells of Williams' journey to the top – stopping off on the way to take a look at his songs, his videos, his shows, his relationships, his rows, his record deals and his demons.